small group bible resources



# Living the kingdom lifestyle

## The Beatitudes

Florence MacKenzie

Scripture Union, 207–209 Queensway, Bletchley, MK2 2EB, England.

email: info@scriptureunion.org.uk
web site: www.scriptureunion.org.uk

We are an international Christian charity working with churches in more than 130 countries providing resources to bring the good news about Jesus Christ to children, young people and families – and to encourage them to develop spiritually through the Bible and prayer.

As well as our network of volunteers, staff and associates who run holidays, church-based events and school Christian groups, we produce a wide range of publications and support those who use our resources through training programmes.



First published 2002

ISBN 1 85999 460 1



British Library Cataloguing-in-Publication Data

A catalogue record for this book is available from the British Library.

Cover design: Carsten Lorenz
Printed in Great Britain by Ebenezer Baylis & Son Ltd, The Trinity Press, Worcester and London.

# Contents

*To James – of all the people I know,*
*you come the closest*
*to living out the principles outlined in this study*
*Thank you for your constant love,*
*your calm strength and your crazy sense of humour.*
*I love you.*

# Introduction

When the idea came to my mind to write a Bible study on the beatitudes, I almost dismissed it. I thought this was a part of the Bible which was so well known that no more could be learned from it. How wrong I was! In writing this study I've been so challenged about my relationship with God and with others – I hope that you will be too.

Many writers have used different ways to portray the beatitudes. Some have used the analogy of a mountain, with the first four beatitudes resembling a climb up the mountain and the second four the descent down from the top. Others have compared them to climbing up a ladder, with one beatitude following the other in an orderly sequence. When I was thinking about this, a very powerful image came to my mind – that of a cross. It seems that the first four beatitudes are mainly concerned with our relationship to God, while the second four deal primarily with our relationships with other people. If the order in which the beatitudes are mentioned is important – and I believe it is – then the first four could be seen as a progressive movement towards God and could therefore be placed on a vertical or upward dimension. The latter four, relating mainly to how we interact with others, could be placed on a horizontal or outward dimension. When the two dimensions are brought together, we have the shape of a cross. It's interesting to see that, when this is done, meekness sits at the intersection of our relationship with God and our relationships with others. I don't think this is accidental.

Why a cross? Well, the cross is central to Christianity because our Lord and Saviour, Jesus Christ, voluntarily died on a cross to save all who believe in him from eternal punishment for their sins. By turning our back on everything which displeases him and trusting in him as the only way to God, we will have eternal life – new life which begins when we become Christian believers and continues after death when we will live in heaven with God forever. There will be no cross in heaven – there doesn't need to be because, when Jesus died on the cross at Calvary, he did all that was necessary to make it possible for you to go there. What are you waiting for? Join me in this study of the beatitudes – I think you'll be glad you did!

# How to use this study

Welcome to the 'Living the Kingdom lifestyle' Bible study. My desire is that as you study and share your findings with others, you will be drawn into a closer relationship with the Lord and will become more and more the person he wants you to be.

This Bible study has two main emphases: the first is to encourage you to dig deep into the word of God because this is our main guide for living, and the second is to help you apply this word to your daily life. Only God's word is completely trustworthy and, if we are going to live in a way which will honour and please him, then we need to know what he says in the Bible. This is the touchstone of all debate. However, being merely familiar with what the Bible says is, in itself, insufficient. In order for God's word to be real and vital, there needs to be application of the truths that we read about there. The best way to do this is to co-operate with the Holy Spirit. Ask him to help you take on board what God is saying to you in the Bible. Ask him to apply his word to you so that there is no way that you can remain unchanged by its power. Biblical truth applied to our lives by the Holy Spirit results in spiritual growth and changed attitudes and behaviour.

This study is for either individual or group application. If you are sharing your answers with others in a group, this is a good way to support and encourage one another. However, the most important part of the study is in preparation. Allow yourself plenty of time to read the questions and the Bible references. Get alone with the Lord and his word. Ask him for his help as you go through each of the questions. Don't concern yourself about 'wrong answers' – do as much as you can, as completely as you can. This is really your learning period. Fully prepared in this way, you will find that you will receive immense benefit from the subsequent sharing in your group. You will also be in a much stronger position to contribute thoughtfully and meaningfully – this will be greatly appreciated by both your leader and other group members.

The time taken in preparation will vary from person to person. Don't be concerned if it takes a while to complete each chapter. My intention is that the questions and Bible verses will cause you to linger in the Lord's presence. However, I suggest you avoid the temptation of answering all the questions from a chapter in one sitting the day or evening before you meet with the rest of your group to share what you have written. It might overwhelm you to tackle a whole chapter at a time. Instead, you will probably find it helpful to divide up each chapter into study sections. For example, each one is already divided into three parts. Depending on the frequency with which your group meets, you might wish to do each section over two days, giving a six day preparation time, with about twenty minutes per day devoted to answering the questions, reading the Bible verses and praying about the application to your own life. This could be a suitable pattern if your group meets every week. On the other hand, if you meet with others every two weeks, you could complete the study by spending around twenty minutes every other day, or by spending less time each day but preparing your answers over a ten or twelve day period. The way you prepare is essentially up to you – different people have different needs and responsibilities – but the important thing is that you develop a pattern of study which works for you and then stick to it! If you haven't approached Bible study in this way before, you will find the discipline involved to be extremely beneficial in your walk with the Lord.

I would be delighted if this study challenged you to examine the way you live as a follower of Jesus and resulted in a lifestyle which is consistent with his teaching in the opening verses of Matthew chapter 5.

# Notes for leaders

Leading a Bible study is a great privilege and responsibility. Not only do leaders need to thoroughly prepare the study material, but they also need to prepare themselves. This involves being in a close relationship with the Lord, arising out of personal Bible study and prayer, along with a commitment to live their lives to God's glory. No matter how much natural talent leaders might have, they are absolutely dependent upon the Lord for wisdom and help in leading their groups. My desire is that, as you study this material together with your group members, you will draw your strength from him and will become more like him.

Encourage your group members to write down their answers to the questions before coming to the Bible study meeting. In my own experience as group leader, and in talking with other leaders, I've found this to be a vital part of Christian growth. Preparation allows an opportunity to be guided by the Holy Spirit in answering the questions, whereas an 'off-the-cuff' response during the meeting, with no prayerful preparation time, is less likely to be helpful to others in the group. Asking that all members of your group prepare each chapter in advance of your meeting helps to encourage timid, less knowledgeable members to contribute their responses on a more equal footing with spiritually mature members – this, in turn, can lead to greater spiritual growth and unity within the group.

This Bible study will take about sixty to ninety minutes to discuss people's answers to the questions. It's important that all questions are covered in your meeting, because if you get into the habit of not discussing the final questions in each chapter, your members might not prepare answers to these questions for future chapters. I suggest, therefore, that you prepare a time schedule in advance of your meeting – write down your start time at the beginning, then the time you expect to complete the first section, and the second section, and finally the third section of the chapter to be discussed. In this way, you should be able to keep track of your time and know whether you need to slow down or speed up in discussing your group's responses.

May the Lord be constantly at your side as you seek to lead others into a deeper knowledge of him.

# 1| Who? How? What?

'Blessed are the poor in spirit, for theirs is the kingdom of heaven. Blessed are those who mourn, for they will be comforted. Blessed are the meek, for they will inherit the earth. Blessed are those who hunger and thirst for righteousness, for they will be filled. Blessed are the merciful, for they will be shown mercy. Blessed are the pure in heart, for they will see God. Blessed are the peacemakers, for they will be called sons of God. Blessed are those who are persecuted because of righteousness, for theirs is the kingdom of heaven. Blessed are you when people insult you, persecute you and falsely say all kinds of evil against you because of me. Rejoice and be glad, because great is your reward in heaven, for in the same way they persecuted the prophets who were before you.'

Matthew 5:3–12

*The Beatitudes are Christ's instruction manual for building a disciple. In them, he describes eight steps to becoming the Christian you always wanted to be ... They'll teach you the most important skills for facing your most challenging spiritual problem – yourself. They'll identify the attitudes necessary for living in the presence of God. They'll educate you in the ways disciples live and deal with other people. They'll help you manage your most intimate relationships ... With eight sure strokes, Jesus paints the portrait of a true believer.*

Tim Woodroof [1]

The beatitudes – or 'beautiful words' – of Matthew 5:1–12 conjure up all sorts of ideas in people's minds. Some might think, 'Oh, yes, they're these nice things which Jesus said on the mountain near the Sea of Galilee.' Or perhaps they say, 'This is Jesus being idealistic – no one could ever attain these principles in practice.' Or maybe they imagine that the beatitudes are for some future time and have nothing to do with us at present. One thing is certain: these are the words of the Son of God, and, therefore, we can't afford to ignore them or misunderstand them. So, let's begin this study by considering, firstly, *who* are the people whom Jesus is referring to; secondly, *how* does he describe them; and thirdly, *what* does he say to them?

## Who are they?

> *What Jesus preached was what we call a 'double-barrelled' sermon. It was crammed with meaning for believers, challenging their lifestyle and testing the depth of their commitment. But it also had a devastating message for unbelievers, shattering their illusions as to the kind of life which is pleasing to God and satisfying to man.*
> John Blanchard [2]

Before we consider who the people are whom Jesus was *specifically* referring to, it's important to give some thought to the groups of people who were in the audience on the day that the Lord's first recorded sermon was delivered.

**Read Matthew 5:1,2; Matthew 7:28,29**

Q Read the verses above and write down who the groups were

Q What might be the purpose in both the disciples and the general crowd hearing this sermon of Jesus?

Q The references above indicate what sort of audience heard Jesus deliver his first public address; but who was he actually describing in verses 3–12 of Matthew 5?

*The beatitudes set forth the balanced and variegated character of Christian people. These are not eight separate and distinct groups of disciples, some of whom are meek, while others are merciful and yet others are called upon to endure persecution. They are rather eight qualities of the same group who at one and the same time are meek and merciful, poor in spirit and pure in heart, mourning and hungry, peacemakers and persecuted. Further, the group exhibiting these marks is not an elitist set, a small spiritual aristocracy remote from the common run of Christians. On the contrary, the beatitudes are Christ's own specification of what every Christian ought to be. All these qualities are to characterise all his followers.*
John R W Stott [3]

A recurring theme throughout chapters 5 to 7 of Matthew's gospel is the need for Jesus' followers to be different from those around them – in attitude, motive, desire, behaviour and character.

**Read 2 Corinthians 5:17; Philippians 4:13; 2 Peter 1:3**

Q Having read the verses above write down the characteristics that make Christians different from those around them.

Q In what way(s) can the above verses help you to identify the people whom Jesus is describing in the beatitudes?

## How are they described?

*In the beatitudes Jesus explains just who are the recipients of God's favour and grace. Not those whom the world sees as successful, but those whose spirits yearn for God. They are the truly blessed ones, and the extent of their blessedness will become fully apparent at the end of the age when the superficiality of the world's standards will*

*be exposed for what they are, and when those whose hearts belong to God are honoured and judged righteous in His kingdom.*
**Ralph F Wilson** 4

The Lord begins each beatitude with the word 'blessed' which has sometimes been translated as 'happy'. However, this doesn't get to the heart of what the word really means. The original Greek word conveys the idea that blessedness is not related to emotions (as happiness is) but rather to character. When the Bible talks about someone being blessed, it's not referring to what they're feeling, but to what they are. I find this so encouraging, don't you? You see, my feelings are forever fluctuating – they rarely stay the same. If being blessed depended on how I felt, I'd be blessed on some days and not on others! If, on the other hand, blessedness refers to my character – what I am – then it's a description of me and I am blessed! In the Bible, blessing involves the idea of imparting or conferring something and denotes favour towards the recipient. God's blessing is always an evidence of his favour and loving concern for us.

**Read Numbers 6:22–26; Psalm 144:15; Luke 1:30,48,49**

Q Having read the references above, what did you learn about blessing from each of them?

Think of ways in which, as a child of God, he has blessed you personally and *take time now* to praise and thank him for these blessings.

Like salvation, God's blessing is not something which we can earn or expect as a right. However, it's been suggested that God's blessing is linked to a Christian's obedience, righteousness and faith.

**Read Matthew 5:6; Luke 11:27,28; John 20:28,29**

Q Why do you think such qualities are related to the blessing of God?

# What was said to them?

> *These beatitudes form* **one** *portrait. When an artist draws a picture, each line may be graceful and masterful, but it is the union of the lines that reveals their mutual relation; it is the combination of the various artistic delineations and minute touches that gives us the complete portrait. So here, though each separate aspect has its own peculiar beauty and grace and shows the hand of a master, it is only when we take all the lines in combination that we get the full portrait of a true subject and citizen in the kingdom of God.*
> **A W Pink** [5]

The message that Jesus delivered to the listeners on the mountainside was truly astonishing. You can just imagine the situation: Jesus sits down and begins to speak. (The fact that he sat down is important – this was the posture of a rabbi or teacher. Jesus' audience knew from this that he had something important to say.) In Jewish literature, the blessed man was the one who had a good wife, obedient children, faithful friends, a prosperous lifestyle etc. The last thing that his Jewish audience expected to hear was that it was the poor in spirit, the mourners, the meek, and so on, who were truly blessed – even more astonishing that they should be the heirs to such wonderful promises. In Jesus' time, as in our own, what he said was considered revolutionary and counter-cultural.

**Read Matthew 5:3–10**

Q Select two beatitudes which you find surprising. Give a reason for your answer.

Notice that, in each of the beatitudes, there is a promised blessing linked to the various characteristics. Using the following table, match up the blessing with the relevant characteristic.

| Characteristic | Promised blessing |
|---|---|
| Poor in spirit | Will inherit the earth |
| Mourners | Will see God |
| Meek | Will be filled |
| Hungry and thirsty | Theirs is the kingdom of heaven |
| Merciful | Will be comforted |
| Pure in heart | Will be called sons of God |
| Peacemakers | Theirs is the kingdom of heaven |
| Persecuted | Will be shown mercy |

Q Do you think that a Christian should have only some of the above characteristics or all of them? Give a reason for your answer.

Q Ask the Lord *now* to make you willing to be changed by his power so that, over the next few weeks as you continue in your study of the beatitudes, you'll begin to show more and more of a resemblance to the portrait painted in Matthew 5:3–10.

## Personal comment

*I'm so thankful that the Lord doesn't expect me to live out the beatitudes by drawing on my own resources, by trying harder or by doing my best – we both know that I would fail miserably! I once heard a story of a little boy who loved playing football. However, he was quite slow in passing the ball to the other players and often missed the ball when it was directed at him. He became rather sad when he thought that he would probably never become a great footballer. As he thought of ways to improve his performance on the football pitch, he thought of his favourite Manchester United player. 'Oh,' thought the little boy, 'if only he could come and live inside me, then every time I went to kick the ball, I'd never miss. I could step to the side and let him take over.' As you begin this study of the beatitudes, are you prepared to step aside and let the One who lives in you take over? The little boy would have to dream on – the Man U player could never live inside him. But, for Christian believers, having a helper live inside them is no dream – the Bible tells us that the Holy Spirit of God lives in every Christian (John 14:17; 1 Corinthians 6:19) and 'the Spirit helps us in our weakness' (Romans 8:26a). As you take time to carefully read through Matthew 5:3–10 it will soon become apparent that, if you rely on your own strength of character to be like the descriptions given there, the verses will appear as unattainable ideals. It's only people who acknowledge their own poverty of spirit and surrender to the power of the Holy Spirit who will be found among those whom Jesus calls 'blessed'. Why not pray something like this? 'Lord, as I read your words, I want you to guide my thinking. Please change my heart and will. I can't live like this if left to myself. I need the help of your Holy Spirit.' If you allow the Lord to work in you, you will begin to see the beatitudes, not as unattainable ideals, but as a portrait of the person God wants you to be.*

# 2| Poor in spirit

'Blessed are the poor in spirit, for theirs is the kingdom of heaven.'
Matthew 5:3

*To be poor in spirit means that we see our total spiritual poverty before God and our utter dependence on Him. Poverty of spirit must be our attitude toward ourselves. We must see that we can do nothing to commend ourselves to God. It must become clear to us that apart from Christ we are spiritually destitute. We may be well educated, but we are spiritually ignorant. We may be financially secure, but we are spiritually bankrupt. We may be the president of a corporation, but without Christ we are on the spiritual unemployment line.*
J David Hoke [1]

Have you ever wished you could get rid of preconceived ideas about what words mean and start from scratch without any distorted interpretations? Would the words *'poor in spirit'* fit into this category? There are lots of views going around as to what this phrase means. Some have suggested that it refers to the financially poor, or the intellectually poor, or those with poor self-esteem and so on. To focus on these interpretations, however, is to miss the whole point of what Jesus was saying. Poverty of spirit has little to do with what we do or don't possess, but a lot to do with our attitude towards these possessions, as well as our attitude towards ourselves and God. As the first point on the upward dimension of the cross, however, it's mainly concerned with our relationship to God. For those who are poor in spirit, Jesus gives an incredible promise – 'theirs is the kingdom of heaven.'

# What does it mean to be poor in spirit?

> *Jesus said, 'Blessed are the poor in spirit; for theirs is the kingdom of heaven'. What does this mean? I believe it means that those who in their spirit see themselves as possessionless are those who are blessed and happy. When a person possesses Jesus Christ and eternal life in heaven, they are the richest of all people. Nothing else can really make us rich except these heavenly possessions.*
> Mary Whelchel [2]

When we think of someone being poor, we imagine a person who has few possessions, has a very low income, and is unable to afford the luxuries of life. The Greek word for 'poor' in Matthew 5:3 goes much further than this – it describes those who are *completely destitute* and, as such, are *totally dependent* on others' goodwill for their survival. It brings out the idea of people being bankrupt, with no resources of their own with which to improve their lot. They are totally and utterly helpless to better themselves. Read the verses below and write down the principal characters in each case. In what way(s) were these people both destitute and dependent?

**Read Mark 12:41–44; Luke 16:19–21; Luke 18:9–14**

Q A biblical example of one who could be described as being poor in spirit can be found in Luke 18:9–14. How did the tax collector demonstrate his poverty of spirit in contrast to the Pharisee?

Q How did the Pharisee demonstrate his pride?

Q Which of the two men went home in a right relationship with God?

Read the second part of verse 14: *'For everyone who exalts himself will be humbled, and he who humbles himself will be exalted.'* Do you exalt yourself or humble yourself? Do you expect God to receive you on the basis of things like your upbringing, social status, good works, etc, or are you prepared to see yourself through God's eyes – as a destitute beggar, a spiritual down-and-out, with nothing to offer him? Even our best acts are like dirty rags in God's sight (Isaiah 64:6) and often things we have done which we are proud of are regarded in a completely different way by him (Revelation 3:17). Do you depend *totally* on his forgiveness and mercy? Be honest with yourself as you take time now to ask the Lord to show you areas in your life where you need to be poor in spirit – then act upon what he says.

## What is the kingdom of heaven?

> *The Kingdom of Heaven is that wonderful kingdom that we enter when we are saved. Our homeland is Heaven when we are born again. And the entrance into Heaven is not on our merit, not by our worthiness, not because we are justly proud of anything that we are. Our entrance into Heaven is because we have become totally aware and have recognized and have admitted the sad fact that we are bankrupt, that we are in terrible trouble with God, and we are ready to throw ourselves on His mercy.*
> Harold Camping [3]

Jesus loved talking about the kingdom of heaven. In Matthew's gospel, he refers to the kingdom more than fifty times. In other gospels, the term 'kingdom of God' is more commonly used. The main reason for this distinction was that Matthew, unlike the other gospel authors, was writing for a predominantly Jewish readership and, to devout Jews, God's name was so holy that they would not utter it – hence, kingdom of heaven. Referring to this kingdom as 'of heaven' or 'of God' indicates its supernatural nature – and it is this kingdom that the Lord promises to those who are poor in spirit.

**Read Acts 1:6; John 18:36**

Q What do these verses tell you about the disciples' view of the kingdom and Jesus' view of the kingdom?

**Read Luke 17:20,21; 2 Peter 1:11**

Q What do these verses say about the kingdom?

Q Every kingdom has a monarch – one who rules. What does it mean for you personally to be under the rule of Jesus Christ now in your everyday life?

Q The kingdom of heaven also has a future aspect to it which will be revealed when Christ returns.

**Read Matthew 25:31–34**

Q What do these verses say about the future nature of the kingdom?

The kingdom of heaven is both a present and a future reality. In Matthew 5:3, Jesus focuses on the current nature of the kingdom by giving a sure promise to the poor in spirit – 'theirs is the kingdom of heaven.' Another way of saying this would be 'theirs *and theirs alone* is...' The kingdom of heaven belongs to all those who are poor in spirit – anyone who is not poor in spirit has no share in this kingdom.

Take time now to consider areas in your life where Jesus is not reigning because you're resisting his right to be Lord over everything. If it helps, write down specific areas where you know you're living contrary to what his Word says; or where you're not prepared to fully trust him with the consequences of decisions which have been made or still need to be made concerning the future. I find the following quote (source unknown) to be very challenging in my own life: 'If he is not Lord of all, then he is not Lord at all.'

# Live It Out!

> *We can be examples to those in our lives who have never heard of being poor in spirit. To those who are looking for answers, looking for peace, but don't realize the only honest answer, the only real peace, comes from being a part of the kingdom of God.*
> Bill and Michael Dodds [4]

We've seen that to be poor in spirit is to realise that we're spiritually bankrupt – we're totally unable to make any payment towards our salvation. Like the poor widow in Mark 12:42, the poor in spirit throw themselves on God's mercy – they become totally dependent on him for salvation and for the power to live today in his kingdom under his rule. The remaining questions and exercises are intended to help you to live out the principles of God's kingdom in your everyday life.

**Read John 15:5b**

Q Do you think that poverty of spirit is necessary only to enter the kingdom (ie at salvation), or should Christians consistently be aware of their own weakness and the need for ongoing dependence on God?

**Read Philippians 4:13**

Q If the confidence of Christian believers is not in themselves, where does their strength come from?

Q What other resources has the Lord given to us?

Admit to God that you are poor in spirit and ask him to keep you like that from day to day. Write this out in the form of a prayer. Refer to it often, amending and extending it as you become more conscious of the need to maintain poverty of spirit.

At this point, you might be wondering how you can *practically* demonstrate poverty of spirit in your daily life. Look up the verses in the list below and in the space provided make a note of the ways in which poverty of spirit is demonstrated.

| Verses | Possible ways to demonstrate poverty of spirit |
|---|---|
| Psalm 40:8 | Delight to do God's will |
| Matthew 7:7 | |
| John 3:30 | |
| Philippians 2:3 | |
| Philippians 2:14 | |
| 1 Thessalonians 5:18 | |
| Hebrews 12:2 | |

Over the next few weeks, use the above inventory to help you to demonstrate poverty of spirit. Add your own suggestions to the list as ideas come to mind.

## Rich rewards

Although the first beatitude illustrates the necessity of poverty of spirit for those who live under the authority and rule of the Lord, the Bible is full of references to the *riches* that are available to these 'poor-in-spirit' people. In the following table, match up the verses with the corresponding riches for those who are in Christ.

| Verses | Blessing |
|---|---|
| Rom 10:12 | God richly provides us with everything for our enjoyment |
| 2 Cor 6:10 | We are to be rich in good deeds |
| 2 Cor 8:9 | We are richly blessed if we call on Him |
| Eph 3:16 | Christ's word lives in us richly |
| Phil 4:19 | We are strengthened by God's riches |
| Col 3:16 | We are able to make others rich |
| 1 Tim 6:17 | We become rich through the Lord's poverty |
| 1 Tim 6:18 | Our needs are met out of Christ's riches |

Choose at least one of the above verses and state specifically how you can apply it in a practical way to your life this week. Be prepared to share this with your group members for their encouragement.

## Personal comment

*If you or I were to write the beatitudes, I wonder how we would start? Perhaps we would say: 'Blessed are the leaders in the church ...' or 'Blessed are the children who go to Sunday School ...' or 'Blessed are those who write Bible studies ...' I doubt if we would say: 'Blessed are the poor in spirit ...' As I resourced material in preparation for writing this study, I was challenged again and again as to what it really meant to be poor in spirit. This is no easy teaching – this isn't something we can take up as a hobby to pass the time and then put away in a drawer when we grow tired of it. In fact, if left to ourselves, we can't even begin to be poor in spirit! We just can't make it on our own. The wayward youth in Luke 15:11–32 couldn't make it on his own either. You might remember how he asked for his inheritance to be advanced to him – as the younger son, he was entitled to a third of his father's wealth while his elder brother was entitled to two thirds. It was acceptable for a father to distribute wealth to his family while he was still alive, but this was normally initiated by the father and not, as in this case, by the son.*

*So, our prodigal got off to a bad start – and that was before he started getting into difficulties! The money didn't last long, of course, and the youth soon found himself in a desperate situation – not only did he work among pigs (unclean animals by Jewish standards), but he was so hungry he wanted to eat the pigs' food! He couldn't sink any lower – he was at rock bottom. Finally, he decided he would seek the mercy of his father. The boy was poor in the real sense of the word – destitute and totally dependent on the goodwill of another. Look at the poverty of spirit evident in verses 18 and 19 – 'I will set out and go back to my father and say to him: Father, I have sinned against heaven and against you. I am no longer worthy to be called your son; make me like one of your hired men.' Did his father grant his request? No. Instead, he welcomed the youth back with open arms and an open heart – this was reason to celebrate! What a picture of the poor in spirit casting themselves totally on the mercy of God the Father and receiving riches direct from the Father's hand. The boy hadn't earned his father's kindness and his elder brother didn't like it.*

*There are those who can't accept that being poor in spirit is the first step to being in a right relationship with God and being in his kingdom – they would love to stand by and watch others struggle and fail to enter in. Entry into such a kingdom, some would say, should be by merit and self-advancement. Yet others would propose that, if such a kingdom exists at all, then there should be no criteria whatever for entry: let everyone in – poor in spirit, proud in spirit. But we are drawn back to the words of Jesus – words spoken early in his public ministry: 'Blessed are the poor in spirit, for theirs is the kingdom of heaven.'*

# 3| Those who mourn

'Blessed are those who mourn, for they will be comforted.'

Matthew 5:4

*What is mourning? It's the realization that failure and sin and guilt can only be addressed by treating them with the seriousness they deserve. Mourning is bitter tears, a broken heart, a burning shame, a cutting guilt. It's weeping, wailing, and grieving. It's sorrow to the point of exhaustion, remorse to the edge of despair. Mourning is a killing pain that demands the death either of the sinner or the sin. It is one of the greatest needs among God's people today.*

Tim Woodroof [1]

Mourning sounds such a dreary word, doesn't it? In some ways, it seems even more unattractive than poverty of spirit. Yet, it's one of the brush-strokes necessary for painting the portrait of a follower of Jesus. Each beatitude builds on the one before and we can't mourn in the way the Lord requires until we acknowledge our poverty of spirit; similarly, poverty of spirit, in itself, is incomplete – it needs to be clothed in mourning. The blessing, of course, lies not in the mourning but in the promise to the mourners – 'they will be comforted'.

## What does it mean to mourn?

*Judas openly acknowledged his sin and even made restitution of the blood money, but it seems clear that he was motivated by fear rather than by anything else, because he never sought forgiveness. Instead, his self-reproach led to a despair which left no room for God's forgiving grace. Whatever emotions may have racked Judas' heart, his was not 'repentance unto life' (Acts 11:18).*

John Blanchard [2]

We've probably all mourned at some point in our lives. We've perhaps mourned the death of someone close to us; mourned the absence of friends; mourned over a friend's difficult circumstances; and so on. But is this the kind of mourning which Jesus is talking about in this beatitude? From the context, it would appear that it's not. We know from both the Bible and personal experience that not all mourners are comforted. An example of someone like this is Judas, the betrayer of Jesus, whose mourning over his wrongdoing arose out of his guilt.

**Read Matthew 27:1–5**

Q Notice in verse 3 that Judas, the betrayer of Jesus, 'was seized with remorse' and in verse 4 said to the chief priests and elders, 'I have sinned.' Were these two things sufficient for Judas to obtain God's forgiveness?

Q What was missing from his response?

Q Judas 'went away and hanged himself' (Matthew 27:5). After denying Jesus, Peter 'went outside and wept bitterly' (Matthew 26:75). Both of these men were responding to guilt – what was the essential difference between the two responses?

Are you deeply sorry because of some specific sin in your life and not just because of its consequences? Has your remorse led to genuine repentance? Have you turned to God and asked him to forgive you for this sin? As well as confessing your sin, do you mourn over it? Take time now to consider each of these questions, asking the Lord to help you to answer appropriately. Genuine sorrow for sin shouldn't be just a one-off response which occurred at the time when you became a Christian – this response should characterise your attitude to sins which you continue to commit.

# What does it mean to be comforted?

*Jesus is pronouncing a blessing on those who are characterised by mourning. He does not mean those who are naturally negative, have a poor self-image, and who are constantly seeing the blackest side of things, but those whose hearts have been so tenderised by the Holy Spirit that they grieve whenever sin raises its ugly, God-dishonouring head.*
John Blanchard [3]

**Read Matthew 5:4; 2 Corinthians 1:3**

Q In Matthew 5:4, mourning is active – 'Blessed are they *who mourn*', while comforting is passive – 'for they *will be comforted*'. Mourning is something we do and the comforting is something done to us. It doesn't come from ourselves, but from 'the God of all comfort' (2 Corinthians 1:3). What encouragement do you receive from this phrase?

The word 'comforted' originally meant to draw alongside someone, often with the effect of strengthening them through encouragement. Those who grieve because of their sin can be comforted and encouraged in several ways. Look at the list below and match up the appropriate verses with who or what offers comfort.

| Verses | Source of comfort |
|---|---|
| John 14:16,17 | Christ as our sacrifice |
| Acts 2:38,39 | The Lord's Supper/Eucharist |
| Romans 15:4 | Fellowship with other believers |
| 1 Corinthians 10:16,17 | Our baptism |
| 1 Thessalonians 4:15–18 | Certainty of Christ's return |
| Philemon v 7 | Word of God |
| 1 John 2:1,2 | God the Holy Spirit |

We can see from the above that comfort is available from several sources.

**Read Psalm 77:1,2, 10–20**

Q Are you surprised that, in the light of his untiring seeking of the Lord, Asaph was still not comforted? Give a reason for your answer.

Q What was missing from Asaph's earlier attitude which is present in verses 13–20?

> *Asaph cried out to God for courage during a time of deep distress … He said, 'I cry out to God.' But in 77:13–20, the I is gone. As Asaph expressed his requests to God, his focus changed from thinking of himself to worshipping God … Only after he put aside his doubts about God's holiness and care for him did he eliminate his distress. As we pray to God, he shifts our focus from ourselves to him.*
> Life Application Study Bible [4]

Are you refusing to be comforted where you are right now? Are you so preoccupied with your distress that your view of God is blurred? Take time now to readjust that focus and to remember what God has done for you in the past and consider the power that is his. I suggest you make a list of words which describe his character and use these terms to give praise to him – yes, praise! This will remind you of the nature of the one to whom you cry out – you can't deal with anyone who is more powerful, compassionate and forgiving than the Lord. In 2 Chronicles 20:12, King Jehoshaphat says to God: 'We do not know what to do, but our eyes are upon you.' Continue to ask the Lord to keep your focus on him.

*Yes, mourning Christians are comforted even now by the Divine Comforter: by the ministrations of His servants, by encouraging words from fellow Christians, and (when these are not to hand) by the precious promises of the Word being brought home in power by the Spirit to their hearts out of the storehouse of their memories.*
**A W Pink** [5]

The following list contains promises of God which can provide great comfort for believers. In the spaces provided write down the promises.

| Verses | Type of comfort |
|---|---|
| Psalm 30:5 | Joy in the morning |
| Isaiah 35:10 | |
| 2 Corinthians 4:17 | |
| Philippians 4:7 | |
| 2 Peter 3:13 | |
| 1 John 1:7 | |
| Revelation 21:4 | |

Q Choose one of the above verses to commit to memory this week. Why have you chosen this particular verse?

Take time now to give thanks to the Lord for his willingness to comfort those whose spirits are crushed because they feel the weight of their sin. Is there anyone known to you to whom the above verses would be a comfort at the present time? Are you prepared to share them with that person? Commit this to the Lord in prayer and trust him to direct you in this matter.

# Live it out!

*Until we set our sights on joy that is based on God and His will, we postpone indefinitely the day when we will know true, consistent joy, joy that does not fluctuate with happenings. Only God is always*

> *good and permanently satisfying. Everything about Him is unchanging and eternal – His love, His power, His throne, His promises. His joy expresses itself in a variety of forms – in restful enjoyment, carefree cheerfulness, jubilant exultation, or quiet expectancy of future delights promised in God's Word. Though the form may vary, the joy can never be quenched.*
> Warren and Ruth Myers [6]

So, comfort is promised to those who mourn over their sins – those who not only acknowledge their sins but who see the seriousness and the vileness of sin to such an extent that they mourn with deep heartfelt remorse. While it's right to mourn over our sin, we should be careful not to become melancholy, always mourning over past sin which has been forgiven. We need to remind ourselves that we've been made clean from our sin and can enjoy the liberating power which is ours as people who are free in Christ. If you've confessed your sin to the Lord and are deeply sorry for it, then accept the forgiveness which he promises (1 John 1:9) and move on in your service for him. But don't forget how awful a thing sin is, in all its forms. The verses below describe the response of the apostle Paul, a mature Christian, to continuing sin in his life.

**Read Romans 7:18,19,24**

Q Having read these verses, summarise the main points in your own words.

As part of living out the principles of God's kingdom, how might you mourn on a practical, day-to-day basis? Read the list which follows and identify all those which you think are relevant.

- Be contrite, be sorry for your sin, hate it, and resolve not to commit that sin again.
- Demonstrate your sorrow in some way, eg fast from food, leisure, sleep, etc
- Pretend that you have no need of mourning
- Ask the Lord for a spirit of repentance.

**Read Psalm 38:18; Jeremiah 8:21–9:1; Luke 5:8; Romans 12:15**

These verses relate the experience of people who loved God and mourned for their sin. Although it's right to mourn over sin, we should also be joyful people. In 2 Corinthians 6:10, Paul says that he was 'sorrowful, yet always rejoicing'.

**Read Psalm 31:7; Isaiah 61:10; Philippians 4:4**

Q In your own words, write down what each of these say about being joyful.

Q Choose one of the above verses which especially appeals to you. Share the reason for your choice with the rest of your group.

# Personal comment

*If I thought being poor in spirit was tough, living a life of mourning seems even less appealing! But if I don't mourn, I won't receive comfort. The emphasis of this beatitude is that those who mourn, and they alone, will be comforted. Therefore, to receive God's comfort in the form of his forgiveness, his presence, his guidance, his assurance, and his joy, then I must mourn; I must treat sin seriously and see it for what it is – vile, filthy and noxious. One Puritan writer described sin as 'the devil's excrement'. Not pleasant, not pleasant at all. It's this 'seeing sin for what it is' that's important here. In 2 Samuel 11, we can read the account of King David's adultery with Bathsheba and his murder of her husband, Uriah. The following chapter tells us about the prophet Nathan going to David, possibly a year after the event. David must have known he had sinned long before Nathan visited him – he was familiar with the ten commandments which condemned adultery and murder. He may even have formally confessed his sin, but it took Nathan's visit to make him* feel *his sin and see it for what it was. Only then could he begin to mourn for that sin (see Psalm 51, especially verses 8, 12 and 17). Have you been satisfied with a mere acknowledgement of sin in your life? Is there some specific sin which you've rationalised and, as a result, it doesn't seem so bad now? When you consider that wrong way of thinking or of behaving, does it produce any revulsion in you or have you learned to accept what God has not? Ask the Lord to give you a spirit of genuine repentance so that you can turn away from that sin and turn towards God for forgiveness.*

*Remind yourself that, as a Christian, you have the Holy Spirit living in you and, if you surrender more and more to his influence in your life, you will become more and more willing to do those things which delight him and less inclined to view sinful practice as an acceptable alternative to living God's way. Do you want the comfort of God and all that that entails? Then ask him to help you to mourn over the sin which is robbing you of the assurance of his love and of a close relationship with him. 'Blessed are those who mourn, for they will be comforted.'*

# 4| The meek

'Blessed are the meek, for they will inherit the earth.'

Matthew 5:5

*It's a shame that we don't use a word that more accurately reflects what Jesus was talking about in his third Beatitude – a pity 'meek' now has such a negative spin to it. Why? Because our time, our society, certainly could use a large dose of meekness. And we would be better off ... if we were more meek.*

**Bill and Michael J Dodds** 1

I've discovered that my American friend, Vicky, uses the same words as I do – however, we don't always mean the same thing. For me, 'jumper' means a sweater, but for her 'jumper' means something resembling a boiler-suit! Identical words can have different meanings, not just across cultures, but through time. One of these time-warped words is 'meekness' – some people nowadays tend to think that meekness is a characteristic of the 'wimp' or the 'doormat' or the person with 'no backbone'. In order to grasp what the Lord really meant when he said 'Blessed are the meek ...', we need to get rid of these distorted interpretations of meekness which have occurred with the passage of time and focus on what the Bible says about this characteristic. Only then will we be able to draw closer to a more accurate understanding of the related promise, '...for they shall inherit the earth'.

## What does it mean to be meek?

*Moses was meek because – knowing full well what he preferred, knowing what he would rather do, knowing his own desires and aspirations – he yielded to the will of God. When what he wanted and what God wanted went in different directions, Moses chose to walk God's way. He learned to say, 'Not my will, but yours be done.'*

**Tim Woodroof** 2

> *Jesus was meek because – knowing what he wanted, clear about what he preferred, aware of what he would like to do – he yielded to the will of God. When what he wanted and what God wanted went in different directions, Jesus took God's way. He, above all men, learned to say, 'Not my will, but yours be done.'*
> Tim Woodroof [3]

Many writers view this characteristic as being solely horizontal in nature – they believe it refers to how we relate to other people. I agree that interpersonal relations are very important, but because of its position between the second and fourth beatitudes, I would suggest that meekness here is primarily vertical – it concerns, to a major extent, our relationship to God. The Greeks used the word that is translated 'meek' to describe horses that had been tamed. The tamed horse didn't lose its strength or become timid, but the strength was harnessed by being brought under the control of its owner, so that the horse no longer exercised its own will, but was obedient to the will of its rider. Only two people in the Bible are described as being meek (NIV 'humble') – Moses in Numbers 12:3 and Jesus in Matthew 11:29. They both exercised this characteristic in submission to God's will – even when this cut across their own personal preferences. Chapters 3 and 4 of Exodus describe Moses' encounter with God at the burning bush.

**Read Exodus 3,4**

Q What are Moses' concerns in the face of the prophecy he is given? What is his plea?

Q How would you describe Moses' response to what God required of him?

**Read Matthew 26:36–46**

Q These verses record Jesus' prayer in the garden of Gethsemane just before his arrest. What is striking about Jesus' first prayer?

Q Having given encouragement to his failing/weakening disciples, Jesus returns to pray. But his prayer has changed. What has happened?

Q Look again at 26:45,46. What is significant about Jesus' words to the disciples upon his final return from the place of prayer?

So, you've acknowledged your spiritual poverty and know that the kingdom of heaven belongs to you. Your mourning over your sins has caused you to run to the Lord for forgiveness and comfort. Of course, like the rest of the beatitudes, being poor in spirit and mourning over our sins should be ongoing processes in our lives. But to what extent have you abandoned your rebelliousness and allowed yourself to be tamed by him? Do you surrender to his will and purposes only when they're in line with your own desires? Are you continually coming to the point where you say regarding all areas of your life, 'Not my will, but yours be done'? Submission to God's will is probably hard for all of us – we love ourselves and our own independence too much to surrender to his purposes without difficulty. But it's worth it – the Lord considers such people, the meek, to be blessed. Take time now to allow him to search your attitudes, motives and desires, and ask him to make you willing to be meek.

> *Put those five qualities – humble, gentle, patient, forgiving, and contented – together with being submissive and flexible before God, and you have the truly meek man, the very opposite of the man who is proud, harsh, angry, revengeful, and ambitious. It is only the grace of God, as it works in us by the Holy Spirit, that can make us thus meek.*
> Charles Spurgeon [4]

An offshoot of being meek before God is that we're better equipped to demonstrate meekness in our relationships with others. Several qualities make up this characteristic. Below are some verses which give examples of meekness. Using one word answers, write down the expression of meekness which is referred to in each verse.

| Verses | Example of meekness |
| --- | --- |
| Ephesians 4:32 | Forgiving |
| 1 Thessalonians 2:7 | |
| 1 Thessalonians 5:14 | |
| Hebrews 13:5 | |
| 1 Peter 5:5 | |

# What does it mean to inherit the earth?

> *After this earth has been purified by fire, after God has burned the works of men to ashes, and after every trace of corrupt humanity has been consumed by the fervent heat, then this earth will be fitted up again, angels will descend with new songs to sing, and the New Jerusalem will come down out of heaven from God in all her glory.*
> Charles Spurgeon [5]

We don't work for what we inherit. Those who inherit property, for example, do so as a result of their relationship to the person who is, or was, the owner of it.

**Read Romans 8:17; 1 Peter 1:3,4**

Q What do these verses tell you about your spiritual inheritance?

**Read Proverbs 30:8,9; Matthew 6:19,20**

Q Legal inheritance usually takes the form of acquiring material possessions in some form or another. Does 'inherit the earth' refer to a promise of material prosperity now? Read and paraphrase the verses above for help in answering this question.

**Read Philippians 4:11,12; 1 Timothy 6:6–10; Hebrews 13:5**

Q Paul taught that 'godliness with contentment is great gain' (1 Timothy 6:6). The verses above offer reasons why we ought to be content. Can you identify why?

**Read 2 Peter 3:13; Revelation 21:1–4**

Q The verses from Philippians, Timothy and Hebrews all suggest a higher good, a more precious inheritance, for the sake of which believers renounce worldly riches. However Peter and Revelation present a glorious vision of that inheritance: write down the way(s) in which these verses encourage you.

On the night of his betrayal Jesus warned the disciples that in this world they would face many troubles, but he promised also that, in spite of them, in him they could have peace (John 16:33). Later Paul wrote to the Corinthians that, in eternal perspective, those same troubles are light and momentary and also that they are 'achieving for us an eternal glory that far outweighs them all' (2 Corinthians 4:16–18). Whatever the challenges we face we can be assured that 'in *all* things God works for the good of those who love him, who have been called according to his purpose' (Romans 8:28). Hoping for what we do not yet have, we wait for it patiently (Romans 8:25). How will taking hold of this promise of your future inheritance affect how you pray?

# Live it out!

> *Rest will come as you learn to adjust to the place in which God has put you, as you joyfully and thankfully adapt to the purpose that He intended.*
> Elisabeth Elliot [6]

I wonder if your view of what it means to be meek has changed! Mine certainly has and, rather than wanting to skirt round the idea that I should be meek, I now find that I want to become *more* meek. Isn't it wonderful that the Spirit of God is so ready to work in our lives, making us more like the people we ought to be?

**Read Matthew 26:45–47**

Q Jesus was ready to do the work prepared for him in the circumstances in which he found himself. What would it mean for you to be meek like him in yours?

**Read Matthew 16:21–25; 26:31–35; John 13:5–8; 18:15–18, 25–27**

Q We've already noted that meekness involves submission to the will and purposes of God. It means saying 'yes' to the Lord's teaching and to the situations into which he brings us. A Bible character who initially found it easier to say 'no' to God's way rather than 'yes' was the apostle Peter. Look at the verses above and write down in each case why Peter was saying 'no'.

Q After Jesus rose from the dead and appeared to his disciples, we read that Peter said 'yes' to the Lord. Part of the conversation between the Lord and Peter is recorded in John 21:15–17. Read verses 15 and 16. To what question was Peter answering 'Yes, Lord'?

Q What does this tell us about the relationship between loving the Lord and meekness? (You might find John 14:15 helpful in giving your answer.)

> *Those who humbly and contentedly trust in Christ learn that every experience – the painful as well as the enjoyable – is intended for their spiritual and eternal good, tailored by an all-wise God for their particular benefit and blessing. Meekness is not looking back and seeing this in retrospect. It is approaching each day, each new set of circumstances, in the settled conviction that, in David's famous phrase, 'Surely goodness and mercy shall follow me all the days of my life…'*
> John Blanchard 7

Is there an area in your experience where you need to stop rebelling against God and turn your 'No way, God!' into 'Yes, Lord'? Are you fighting against his purposes for you and, as a result, you are being robbed of the peace, contentment and assurance that can only be yours as you accept with thankfulness his way for your life? Does meekness, properly understood, characterise your relationships with others? The Lord promises that the meek are blessed. Are you?

## Personal comment

*These beatitudes are getting pretty close to the bone, aren't they? They're like a spotlight being shone inside me, illuminating areas of my life which are not surrendered to the Holy Spirit's control. In one sense, it's almost easier for me to hide behind the popular definition of meekness – being soft, weak, or deficient in courage, rather than face up to what a biblical study of meekness reveals. It's not easy being meek – do you want to relinquish your own will and 'rights'? Do you want to say to God 'Not my will, but yours be done?' Do you really want to resist the temptation to retaliate when you're wronged and insulted? We might not want that, but the Lord wants that for us. One of my favourite Bible characters is Jonah – I can identify with him so much. God told him to do something, he didn't want to obey, so he went off in the opposite direction. Are you beginning to identify with Jonah yet? His disobedience caused difficulty for other people and it was only when he had no option but to spend three days inside a fish (are you still identifying with him?) that he was prepared to submit to God's purposes for him. He obeyed God, but then wasn't happy with the outcome. I sometimes feel like that – I believe I've submitted to what God wants me to do, but then I don't like the way things turn out. Surely God has a duty to 'reward' me for good behaviour? Can he not see that submitting to his will was very hard for me – is submission not enough? Must the consequences of obedience sometimes be hard to bear too? But then, if I look at Jesus, the initial consequences of his obedience to his Father's will in Gethsemane were repulsive – a mock trial; wrong accusations; lashed with metal-tipped leather whips that ripped out his flesh; forced to carry the weight of his cross in his physically weakened state; nailed to that cross; stripped of all his clothes; exposed to public humiliation and contempt; the sinless One becoming 'sin for us' (2 Corinthians 5:21); the unimaginable agony of being forsaken by his Father. These were the consequences of Jesus' meekness, his obedience to his Father's will. In Matthew 11:29, Jesus says, 'Take my yoke upon you, and learn of me; for I am meek and lowly in heart ...' (King James Version). We don't know all the consequences that might result if we are meek, but the Lord has promised us that we will be blessed – highly favoured in his sight. Is this enough for me? Is it for you?*

# 5| Those who hunger and thirst for righteousness

'Blessed are those who hunger and thirst for righteousness, for they will be filled.'

Matthew 5:6

*... no man ever becomes hungry and thirsty for righteousness unless he has first passed through the three preliminary stages and has been convinced of his soul poverty, has been made to mourn for sin, and has been rendered humble in the sight of God.*

**Charles Spurgeon** 1

The young mum called to her ten-year-old, 'Eating all that junk will ruin your appetite!' Sure enough, when dinner-time came round, he picked at his meal, leaving more on the plate than in his stomach. Having eaten a bag of crisps and two bars of chocolate not long before his meal meant the boy wasn't hungry for nutritious, wholesome food. Are you hungry for the right things? In the words of the fourth beatitude, do you hunger and thirst for righteousness, or are you filling yourself up with so much junk that it's taken the edge off your appetite for God? As a result, are you feeling empty and dissatisfied? It doesn't have to be like that – Jesus promised that those who hunger and thirst for God, and for the things which please God, will be filled.

# What does it mean to hunger and thirst for righteousness?

> *A blessed person is not one who seeks merely to perform a few acts of righteousness here and there, not one who desires only a part of the righteousness of Christ, but who wants all that is to be had of Christ ... Unfortunately, many Christians desire only part of the righteousness of God in Christ. They want to lead lives of compromise. With one part of their natures they desire sin, and with the other the righteousness of Christ. However, our degree of blessedness, we are told in this Beatitude, depends on how much of the righteousness of Christ we earnestly desire. The more satisfied we become with the righteousness of Christ the more we shall desire it. And the more we desire it the more of it we shall have.*
> Spiros Zodhiates [2]

Matthew 5:6 speaks of 'those who hunger and thirst' and not 'those who are hungry and thirsty'. This highlights the active nature of pursuing righteousness. After acknowledging their spiritual bankruptcy, mourning the seriousness of sin in their lives, and making every effort to continually bring their wills into line with the will and purposes of God, Christian believers are now blessed if they hunger and thirst for righteousness.

**Read Matthew 5:6**

Q Very briefly, what do you think is meant by 'righteousness' here?

**Read Psalm 42:1,2; 63:1; 84:2**

Q In the original Greek, the fourth beatitude refers to hungering and thirsting for as much righteousness as it is possible to have. This kind of appetite is reflected in some of the psalms. Referring to the psalms above, select the words or phrases that indicate the longing that the writers were experiencing.

Q Choose one of the above references to incorporate into your prayer time this week and share with your group the reasons for your choice.

**Read Jeremiah 20:9; Philippians 3:7,8**

Q In Jeremiah 23:6, we read of 'the Lord Our Righteousness' – a reference to the Messiah who would come into the world – our Lord Jesus Christ. In essence, hungering and thirsting for righteousness means nothing less than longing passionately for God himself. The psalmists were not the only ones who demonstrated such longing. In the references above, who or what is the object of the writers' passion?

Q Can you relate an occasion when you felt like Jeremiah or the apostle Paul? If not, how might you encourage others in your group to develop a passion like theirs?

*It's only when we hunger and thirst for righteousness that we are promised to be blessed and filled. God is not trying to make our lives miserable. Rather he knows what will satisfy us and doesn't want us to spoil our appetite for the good stuff – him and his righteousness – by settling for the junk food and the things that never will meet our needs … What's spoiling your appetite for God?*
Mary Whelchel [3]

# What does it mean to be filled?

*The Christian who does not daily hunger for his spiritual bread, and daily ask for it, is likely to starve. He will find no freezers in the Kingdom of God. He doesn't need them. The Lord taught us to pray,*

*'Give us this day our daily bread.' Yesterday's prayer will not do for today, nor today's for tomorrow. Every day, night and day, must he who is in earnest in hungering and thirsting for the sacred food of righteousness, seek it, gather it, and feed upon it for his soul's health.*
Spiros Zodhiates 4

Don't you just love the feeling of satisfaction you get when you've had a good meal and no longer feel hungry? Or the pleasure of a long, cool, iced drink after working in the heat? It feels good to have hunger appeased and thirst quenched, and we should never forget to thank God for the food and drink which he provides for us. In Exodus 16 we read the fascinating account of how the Lord provided food – quail and manna – for the Israelites in the desert.

**Read Exodus 16:4**

Q In sending the manna, God gave instructions about how it was to be gathered. Write down the instruction God gave in Exodus 16:4.

**Read Exodus 16:17–20**

Q Whenever God gives a command, it will either be obeyed or disobeyed – this one was no exception. In the passage above, note the two responses to the above command.

Q What spiritual lesson(s) can be learned from this?

**Read Luke 1:53**

Q Whom does the Lord fill? The Lord doesn't do things by half-measures – he loves to *fill* his people with what he knows they need.

**Read Romans 15:13**

Q What is the purpose of his filling?

**Read Philippians 1:11**

Q To what end does he fill us?

The Lord longs to fill us with even more – for example, Psalm 71:8 talks about being filled with God's praise; Psalm 126:2 about being filled with laughter; Ephesians 5:18 about being filled with the Spirit; and Colossians 1:9 about being filled with the knowledge of his will.

Take time now to thank God that it is possible for you not only to sample some of these blessings, but to be *filled* with them.

Filling is proportional to your spiritual appetite – the more you hunger and thirst, the more you will be filled. Paradoxically, the more you are filled, the more you will continue to hunger and thirst! This is the way the Lord has planned for us to grow spiritually and to become more like him. There will come a time, however, when hunger and thirst will no longer be our experience. When that happens, our filling will be complete and eternal.

**Read Revelation 7:16,17**

Q Write down why we will never again hunger or thirst.

**Read Psalm 17:15**

Q Ultimate satisfaction or fulfilment is described for us here. In what way(s) does this verse encourage you?

> *God will provide for his children's needs in their eternal home where there will be no hunger, thirst, or pain, and he will wipe away all tears. When you are suffering or torn apart by sorrow, take comfort in this promise of complete protection and relief.*
> Life Application Study Bible [5]

# Live it out!

> *O God, I have tasted Thy goodness, and it has both satisfied me and made me thirsty for more. I am painfully conscious of my need of further grace. I am ashamed of my lack of desire. O God, the Triune God, I want to want Thee; I long to be filled with longing; I thirst to be made more thirsty still. Show me Thy glory, I pray Thee, that so I may know Thee indeed. Begin in mercy a new work of love within me.*
> A W Tozer [6]

Hungering and thirsting for *righteousness* is probably not one of society's top ten activities. Make a list of things which people are generally more likely to hunger and thirst for.

# Life-changing ideas

Do you have a craving for any of the items mentioned on your list? Does your appetite for this overtake your desire for righteousness? Do you need to take steps to remedy this situation? Be honest as you answer each of these questions.

In the first section of this study, you were asked to give a brief definition of righteousness. Which of the following might be examples of righteous behaviour? Put a tick beside all those that apply.

- Meeting regularly with other Christians to share what God is doing in your lives.

- Meeting a friend for coffee to catch up on the latest gossip about her neighbour's adulterous affair.
- Making it a priority to have a daily unbreakable appointment with God to read his Word.
- Using the Lord's prayer in Matthew 6:9–13 as a model for your own prayers.
- Waiting until the boss is out of the office before making a long distance phone call to your sister just so you can both have a chat.
- Praying that the Lord would turn your 'taste' for him into a 'hunger and thirst' for him and his commands.

Do any of the above actions need to be eliminated from your life because they are dulling your hunger and thirst for righteousness? Are there any other actions not mentioned above which are having the same effect? If so, what steps do you plan to put into action to deal with this?

From the list of actions which you ticked as 'righteous', choose one (to start with) that you can begin working on right away. How do you intend to put this into practice?

Share this plan with the rest of your Bible study group for everyone's encouragement. You might wish to pray with and for each other as you begin, with the Lord's help, to put your plan into action. Be aware that new habits (especially good ones!) take time to become established – perseverance is the order of the day!

## Personal comment

*Do you love food? I do! In fact, I love it so much that I often eat things which are not good for me. You know what I mean – high calorie, high fat, high cholesterol junk. Such 'foods' usually taste wonderful and almost instantly increase my blood sugar level so I feel great – great, that is, until I step on the scales and read a weight figure that is much too high for my height and build. Then, it's decision time. Yes, I will make a determined effort to lose weight. I find one of those diet books that tell me I won't really be on a diet at all (am I expected to believe that?) but will merely be eating healthily. So, I give it a try – after all, it will be nice to be able to fit again into some of the clothes hanging in my wardrobe. Day one of 'eating healthily' begins. Will I be able to get through the day without my mid-morning cream bun? I do survive and make it into day two, then day three, and so on, until I find myself at the end of week one of 'eating healthily' (I'm not on a diet, remember). I start on week two and manage very well, I think – after all, these two chocolate bars won't register on the scales, will they? Week three begins and ends, followed by week four. Yes, there have been lapses when I did eat some of that 'junk' I mentioned earlier but, on the whole, this 'eating healthily' has got a lot going for it. Not only am I several kilograms lighter than I was a month ago, but I'm actually beginning to enjoy what I'm eating. I don't have the same craving for chocolate that I used to have (although it hasn't completely gone away!); in fact, my taste is changing.*

*Do you see the parallel with what we've been looking at in this chapter? When I make it a priority to eat food that's good for me, I consume a healthy physical diet; when I make it a priority to live in a way that is right in God's sight, I consume a healthy spiritual diet – daily Bible reading and prayer. As I continue to eat what is good for me, I begin to develop a taste for that food; as I continue to live in a way that is right in God's sight, I begin to develop a taste for that. The more I continue with my new healthy eating habits, the more of a hunger I develop for healthy food and the less appetite I have for the old junk; the more I continue with my new righteousness-seeking habits, the more of a hunger I develop for God and for his priorities in my life and the less appetite I have for those habits which were damaging my spiritual health.*

*Make a start* now *on your action plan which you outlined a few pages ago. When I make up my mind to lose weight, I always have to deal with the temptation to do it* later *– yes, I'll do it, but not yet; perhaps in a week or two. Sounds familiar? The same temptation will no doubt arise when you make the decision to pursue God and good things. Begin today and persevere – you have the help of friends in your study group, but even more precious, you have the help of the Holy Spirit. Ask him always to keep you on course and to increase your hunger and your thirst for all that is right and you can be encouraged in the process because Jesus said, 'Blessed are those who hunger and thirst for righteousness, for they will be filled.'*

# 6| The merciful

'Blessed are the merciful, for they will be shown mercy.'

Matthew 5:7

*Mercy is an eagerness to say, 'Let me help you.' It's the capacity to see the pain of others, to feel for people in pain, and to take active measures to alleviate that pain. Mercy does what it can, when it can, for whomever it can.*

Tim Woodroof [1]

There's a certain appeal to hungering and thirsting for righteousness that makes me want to stay at the fourth beatitude. I'm enjoying being filled by God and I've found I want to know more and more of him. Surely the best way to do that is to end my beatitude journey now, at the pinnacle of the upward beam of the cross. But ... my portrait isn't finished yet – in fact, it's only half done. I still have another four beatitudes to go. It's as if Jesus is nudging me and telling me that it's time to move in a different direction – a horizontal one this time – where my passion for God is to be translated into compassion for people. 'Blessed are the merciful, for they will be shown mercy.'

## What does it mean to be merciful?

*The heresy of justification by works ... says that there are two ways of getting right with God, one through faith in Christ and the other through the merits of our own humanitarian service. Quite apart from going against the grain of everything the Bible teaches, this would produce the absurd scenario in which, for example, a doctor who was an atheist would be brought into a right relationship with a God in whom he did not even believe. Nothing could make it clearer that the Beatitudes are not to be seen as keys for unlocking the door of the kingdom of heaven.*

John Blanchard [2]

Mercy is part of God's character. In 2 Corinthians 1:3, we read, 'Blessed be the God and Father of our Lord Jesus Christ, the Father of mercies and God of all comfort' (NASB).

Mercy has two main elements to it: forgiveness and compassion for those in need. Compassion goes beyond mere sympathy – if it is genuine, it will result in action. There is no better illustration of mercy in action than the life of Jesus. Read the verses below, correctly matching them with the people to whom he showed mercy. Beside the appropriate people, write down the way in which the mercy was shown. The first one is done for you.

| Verses | Mercy shown to | How |
|---|---|---|
| Matthew 9:1–8 | Soldiers at the cross | Prayed for their forgiveness |
| Matthew 15:21–28 | Widow | |
| Matthew 17:14–18 | Crowd of 5000 | |
| Matthew 20:29–34 | Blind men | |
| Mark 1:40–42 | Woman who anointed Jesus' feet | |
| Mark 6:34–44 | Demon-possessed boy | |
| Luke 7:11–15 | Criminal | |
| Luke 7:36–50 | Canaanite woman | |
| Luke 23:34 | Adulterous woman | |
| Luke 23:38–43 | Leper | |
| John 8:1–11 | Paralysed man | |

Q From these examples, what do you learn about Jesus' priorities?

From the exercise above it can be seen that Jesus showed mercy to people in various ways. They were healed, fed, taught, forgiven and raised to life. This is an example of the Lord being concerned with the whole person.

**Read Matthew 4:23,24**

Q Here Jesus addressed mind, spirit and body. What can the Lord's example teach you about the way you show mercy to others?

Some people might argue that this beatitude teaches that anyone can work their way into God's favour if they're kind and compassionate to others. I think we need to remember that the beatitudes were addressed primarily to Jesus' disciples. As twenty-first century disciples or followers of Jesus, they're also addressed to us. As Christians, we've received mercy from God by being forgiven and brought into a right relationship with him. One way we respond to this mercy is by being merciful to others. This doesn't *make* us right with God – but it's one way that we can show that we already *are* right with him. Even the most merciful person on earth cannot earn their salvation by demonstrating mercy.

**Read Ephesians 2:8–10**

Q Paraphrase what these verses say.

Are you relying on your own acts of compassion and kindness to save you? Do you believe that you can 'buy' your entrance into heaven by the good things you do? God is showing his mercy to you right now by drawing your attention to what he has said in the Bible about this important matter. If this is a concern to you, then speak to your group leader who will show you how you can begin a right relationship with God.

# What does it mean to be shown mercy?

> *This parable describes acts of mercy we all can do every day. These acts do not depend on wealth, ability, or intelligence; they are simple acts freely given and freely received. We have no excuse to neglect those who have deep needs, and we cannot hand over this responsibility to the church or government. Jesus demands our personal involvement in caring for others' needs (Isaiah 58:7).*
> Life Application Study Bible [3]

**Read Proverbs 11:25; Matthew 6:14; Luke 6:38**

Q We've seen that being merciful can't buy salvation, but God says that the merciful will be shown mercy. For each of the verses above note the promise to those who consider the needs of others.

Giving and receiving mercy also has eternal relevance. In Matthew 25:31–46, Jesus gives a sobering account of the final judgement. As King and Judge, he puts the 'sheep' on his right and the 'goats' on his left. The sheep are the righteous (right-with-God) ones who recognised their need of salvation during their earthly lives, and the goats are the unrighteous (not-right-with-God) ones who rejected God's way of salvation.

**Read Matthew 25: 34–46**

Q Why are the sheep blessed? Answer from verse 34 only.

Q List the needs mentioned in verses 35,36 (and again in verses 42,43).

Q Both sheep and goats had seen the various needs. How had the sheep responded?

Q How had the goats responded?

Q Why did they both show surprise in the questions they asked the Lord? (Verses 37–39 and 44.)

Q What do you learn from the King's answer? (Verses 40 and 45.)

Q How does this influence your view of acting compassionately to those in need?

## Live it out!

We saw at the beginning of this chapter that being merciful is part of God's character. As his children, we ought to reflect the family likeness and be merciful too. One way which might help you to get going on this is to read

Colossians 3:12–14. This is one of my favourite passages of Scripture which gives a beautiful description of what Christians should be like in their relationships. These don't come naturally; we are told to 'clothe' ourselves with them (verse 12). Without these qualities, we may as well be naked! What words in this passage are relevant to our study of the fifth beatitude?

I've chosen 'compassion' and 'forgiveness' as these were elements of mercy which were highlighted in the first section of the chapter.

## Compassion

> *Opportunities to show mercy to others surround us. There are lonely people in hospitals and nursing homes. Families struggling with financial difficulties need food, clothes, and cash for their rent. Elderly neighbours may be unable to till their gardens or shovel snow ... Those who are discouraged could be lifted up by a note or phone call, no matter how lacking in eloquence. The new person at church would feel welcomed by an invitation to dinner. The young widow and her kids might be thrilled to be included in your family picnic in the park. The non-Christian couple down the block would be delighted to receive a jar of your freshly-made preserves. The list is endless because God's Spirit can always come up with fresh ideas if we are open to Him.*
> **Kathy Johnston** [4]

Compassion involves putting yourself in someone else's shoes – and then doing something about what you find there.

Some examples of compassionate behaviour might include calling in with a casserole for a new work colleague who is recovering from a broken leg; or sharing your faith with a family member with gentleness and respect. Can you think of other examples of compassionate behaviour?

Think of someone you know who is in need. What would it mean for you to show the compassion of Christ to this person? What would it look like?

Are you prepared to go ahead now and *show* compassion towards the person you have been thinking about? You might find it helps you to write down in your diary a specific time when you will do this – otherwise, it might end up that your good intentions don't get any further than just that.

## Forgiveness

> *When a Christian shows mercy, he experiences liberation. He is set free from grudges that drain the strength and unsettle the mind … The most miserable prison in the world is the prison we make for ourselves when we refuse to show mercy. Our thoughts become shackled, our emotions chained, the will is almost paralysed … How thrilling it is to go through life sharing God's mercy and not having to judge people to see if they are 'worthy' of what we have to offer. We stop looking at the externals and begin to see people through the merciful eyes of Christ.*
> Warren W Wiersbe [5]

Colossians 3:13 talks about clothing ourselves with forgiveness. If we forgive, it's not only the offender who benefits. Forgiving others sets us free from the horrible effects of harbouring grudges, or holding on to bitter, resentful feelings and it puts an end to any thoughts of revenge.

**Read Matthew 18:21–35**

Q This passage tells about the enormous debt which a servant owed to his king … What is the main lesson of this parable as it applies to us today?

Q Why should we forgive others?

# Personal comment

*My portrait is now more than half finished. The Master-Artist started with the dark tones of poverty of spirit and deep sorrow for sin as his colour base. On top of this he added the strong strokes of meekness, highlighted with hunger and thirst. He has now begun to enter some detail into the painting – detail regarding how I should interact in my relationships with others. The fine lines of mercy are drawn and the painting begins to take on a three-dimensional quality. But what is mercy? 'Mercy is God letting me off the hook.' So writes Mary Whelchel in her book,* If You Only Knew.[6] *She goes on to say:*

> *Because Jesus paid the price I owed for my sins through His death on Calvary, God is free to be merciful to me and not demand of me what I owe. His holiness cannot be violated by simply overlooking my sins; atonement is essential. So Jesus paid the price and now God can and does show mercy to me.*

*As a Christian, I've experienced that mercy. What the Lord now wants me to do is to show mercy to others. The two strands of mercy – compassion and forgiveness – are essential details of the portrait which the Lord paints in Matthew chapter 5. How obvious are they in my life? If I show mercy at all, is it with the right attitude? Micah 6:8 says that I should love mercy. At the end of Romans 12:8, I'm encouraged to show mercy cheerfully. This indicates that my attitudes are as important as my actions. Let me ask you something: do you find it relatively easy to be compassionate and kind to the people you like – those who are easy to love? What about those you don't like, or those who don't deserve you to be merciful to them? This is where the crunch comes, isn't it? The Bible often helps us get things into perspective and it comes to our rescue here, too. Romans 5:8 says that it was while we were still sinners that Christ died for us. He didn't wait until we were attractive, respectable people before he was compassionate and forgiving towards us. What will our response be to the unloveable people around us? Is our passion for God (previous chapter) big enough to drive us to compassion for others? Talk to God about it, and make sure you listen for his reply.*

# 7| The pure in heart

'Blessed are the pure in heart, for they will see God.'

Matthew 5:8

*True biblical purity is a liberating experience rather than a confining one. It is not a set of hurdles to overcome but a freedom to be embraced.*

**Gary L Thomas** [1]

The woman in my Bible study group turned to me and said, 'With that guy, what you see is what you get.' She recognised his sincerity, integrity and absence of hypocrisy in his relationships. His life was so genuine, you could turn him inside out and you wouldn't find double standards – just transparent honesty. What he was on the outside reflected what he was like on the inside. He wasn't perfect, but I think he might be an example of the kind of person Jesus was thinking about in the sixth beatitude – the pure in heart. Sounds too good to be true? I don't think so because, you see, Jesus knew that it was possible for a person to be pure in heart – otherwise, he wouldn't have said that this kind of individual is blessed (Matthew 5:8). In this chapter, we'll try to get to grips with what it actually means to be pure in heart; then look at how we can understand the promise of seeing God; and, finally, take on board what we've learnt so that it makes a practical difference to the way we live.

## What does it mean to be pure in heart?

*How few of us live one life and live it in the open! We are tempted to wear a different mask and play a different role according to each occasion. This is not reality but play-acting, which is the essence of hypocrisy. Some people weave round themselves such a tissue of lies that they can no longer tell which part of them is real and which is make-believe.*

**John Stott** [2]

Some of you might be thinking 'Does this mean I have to be perfect? I know I'm not perfect, so this beatitude can't be for me.' No, it does not mean that you must be perfect. We read in 1 John 1:8 'If we say we have no sin, we are only fooling ourselves and refusing to accept the truth' (NLT). Then comes the wonderful promise in verse 9 'But if we confess our sins to him, he is faithful and just to forgive us and to cleanse us from every wrong' (NLT).

The beatitudes were originally addressed to people who had been brought up in a Jewish environment. They would have been familiar with the various ceremonial practices which resulted in external purity or cleanliness. Jesus was going further than this, however, by introducing the necessity of being 'pure *in heart*'. We noticed earlier in the study that the order of the beatitudes is significant, with the first four referring primarily to our relationship with God and the second four to our relationship with people. If this is so, then this beatitude must refer to how we relate to others. Look again at the description of the pure-in-heart man in the opening paragraph of this chapter. With this image in mind, read the following verses from the Psalms and select the words or phrases which describe this kind of person.

**Read Psalm 24:3,4; 32:2; 51:6; 86:11**

Q How might a person with these characteristics relate to others?

Q How genuine are you in your relationships with other people? Is there sometimes a mismatch between what you think about them and how you behave towards them? If so, does this cause you concern? As you consider these questions, you might find it helpful to pray Psalm 139:23,24.

In addition to sincerity and lack of hypocrisy in our relationships, being pure in heart also involves sexual purity. We may be living a morally acceptable life in the eyes of those around us, but this beatitude goes deeper than external realities. It dares us to examine what no other person on earth sees – our thought life. Read the following selection of verses and write down what each one says about the way we think.

**Read Proverbs 23:7; Matthew 5:27,28; Philippians 4:8**

Q Choose one of the above references and say how it could help you to keep your thoughts pure. You might find the King James Version helpful here.

*Can you imagine the problems, heartaches, broken homes and relationships, pain, and suffering that could have been totally avoided if the people involved had learned the principle of thinking only what is pure? Purity of thought and mind leads to a life free from guilt and destruction.*
Mary Whelchel [3]

## What does it mean to see God?

*People who live the Beatitudes see God. They see his hand at work in their lives. They see his face in their prayers. They see his likeness growing within them. The Beatitudes are a door disciples enter into the presence of God. They're a lens that brings a distant God near. They're a certificate, authenticating the disciple's gazing rights. They're a seam between the physical and the spiritual, a crack that the invisible God can be seen through. That's why you ought to screw up your courage and commit yourself to the Beatitude lifestyle. Seeing God is worth any risk or hazard there may be.*
Tim Woodroof [4]

Several years ago an astronaut returned from a space mission and said, 'I didn't see God.' Of course, as an unbeliever, he didn't expect to see God and this statement was nothing more than his attempt to dispute God's existence. Jesus promises, however, that the pure in heart *will see God*. The word in the original Greek suggests the idea of gazing with open-eyed wonder and is linked to having a close, intimate relationship with the

Lord. The Bible gives Christians the wonderful promise that, one day, they will see God completely and perfectly.

**Read John 17:24; 1 Corinthians 13:12; 1 John 3:2; Revelation 22:3,4**

Q Write down what each of these verses says about seeing God.

Q If you were asked to commit one of the above verses to memory this week, which would it be, and why?

Whilst 'no one has ever seen God', 'except the one who is from God', Jesus, 'who is at the Father's side, has made him known' (John 1:18 and 6:46). Revealed to us in the life of Jesus (John 14:9) and made known to us by his Spirit (Jeremiah 31:33,34) and in his Word (Luke 24:25–27), we can know him. Other ways are given in the verses below. Match up the verses with the appropriate examples.

| Verses | How we can know God |
|---|---|
| 2 Chronicles 20:17 | By becoming more like the Lord |
| John 4:23,24 | In and through our circumstances |
| Romans 8:28,29 | Intimate fellowship with God |
| 2 Corinthians 3:18 | By being obedient to what he commands |
| 1 John 1:3 | By worshipping with a pure heart |

Are you seeing God rather dimly in any of the above examples? What steps do you plan to take to sharpen your vision? Be as honest and specific as you can.

# Live it out!

> *If you're wrestling with this sin (entertaining impure thoughts), consider how you're seeing God and others. Do you believe God is capable of meeting your needs? Are you carving out time to know Him in increasing intimacy through His Word and prayer? How are you looking at other people? Are you seeing them as image bearers of God or treating them as objects? Are you sharing your heart with others, letting them see your struggle, and receiving the gift of their prayers and willingness to listen? Or are you in hiding?*
> Adam R Holz [5]

The Lord has a wonderful way of getting to the core of things, hasn't he? As Christians, we probably all know the importance of living morally acceptable lives, but how many of us 'go through the motions' of purity – our outward behaviour doesn't break any obvious moral code but we would curl up with shame if anyone knew the thoughts which we're happy to entertain in private. 'It's all part of being human,' you say. 'As long as he doesn't know that I think he's a jerk, then I can carry on praising him to his face.' Someone else might say 'It's OK for me to fantasise about my friend's husband because, well, I would never actually begin an affair with him … would I?' Let's remind ourselves that Jesus said 'Blessed are the pure in heart' – he cuts through all the pretence to what we're really like inside.

**Read Philippians 4:8**

Q This is a verse which continues to challenge me about the way I think. Why not write it out for yourself?

Here we have a direct command to think about things which are true, noble (or honourable), right, pure, lovely, admirable, excellent or praiseworthy. I'm afraid my thinking doesn't always correspond to these requirements. I might think a true thought, eg the girl at the supermarket checkout is very slow, but thinking that she is 'brain-dead' would not be an honourable thought. Philippians 4:8 also includes a command to think pure thoughts.

Q Why is pure thinking important?

Q What are some of the consequences of impure thinking?

This week, begin to memorise Philippians 4:8. Once you've done this, set aside one day to consciously test your thinking against the principles in this verse. Were there any thoughts which didn't conform to Philippians 4:8? Does this concern you at all? If so, let the Lord know of your desire to have your thinking brought into line with biblical principles and ask him to make you more and more conscious of when your thoughts are operating outside the boundaries of this verse. Your wrong thinking patterns will not be removed overnight, but will need to be worked at on a daily basis. However, the more you desire to change the way you think, and depend on the Lord for help in this, the more your thinking will reflect Philippians 4:8. (For further help in applying Philippians 4:8, I highly recommend Mary Whelchel's book *What Would Jesus Think?* It is a biblical and practical consideration of this verse and is very readable.)

In this chapter, we've looked at two aspects of being pure in heart. Firstly, we considered purity of heart as being sincere, honest, genuine, and not hypocritical or false. Examples of a desire to be pure in heart could include praying Psalm 26:2 because you want to be right in God's eyes; or pointing out to a shop assistant that he has given you a £10 note in change instead of a £5 note. Can you think of additional examples of what it might mean to be pure in heart?

Being pure in heart also means keeping a close check on our sexual thoughts and desires. There's nothing wrong in married people having thoughts about sex with their partner, but when these thoughts are extended to someone outside of that relationship, then they become impure and sinful. How, then, do we keep our thoughts pure? Match up the following verses with examples of ways to avoid impure thinking.

| Verses | Ways to avoid impure thinking |
|---|---|
| Romans 12:1,2 | Trust God's faithfulness |
| 1 Corinthians 10:13 | Be honest with other Christians |
| 2 Timothy 1:7 | Change the way you think |
| James 5:16 | Be disciplined |

Another way of resisting impure thoughts is by doing all that you can to avoid potential sources of temptation. This means avoiding any kind of pornography; staying away from television programmes, videos or films which give a distorted and unbiblical view of sex; and refusing to read books or magazines which would pollute your thinking.

You may be struggling with impure thoughts, as many Christians do, but this is a serious issue and if you continue to entertain these thoughts, you are living at less than God's best for you. Is there a Christian whom you can trust to help you work through this? If not, you might wish to speak to your Bible study leader who may be able to direct you to someone who can help.

## Personal comment

*As a psychologist, I'm fascinated by the human mind and the way we think. A huge amount of work has been carried out into how we process information through our senses and how we then translate that information into thoughts. A lot of valuable discoveries have been made in psychological research but there is so much that we have yet to understand because we are such complex, unique beings. The Bible has quite a lot to say about our minds and thoughts too. The first part of Romans 12:2 says, 'Do not conform any longer to the pattern of this world, but be transformed by the renewing of your mind'. Is there so much filth and rubbish in your mind that you would gladly exchange it for a new one which is pure? Well, you can have a new mind if you allow God to transform you by changing the way you think. Ephesians 4:23 has a similar emphasis and talks about being 'made new in the attitude of your minds'. Furthermore, at the end of 1 Corinthians 2:16, we read '... we have the mind of Christ'. Do you see how awesome this is? Christ, by his Spirit, lives in us if we are Christians and we can therefore think like he does! The devil would like us to believe that we have no alternative but to think thoughts which are selfish, angry, impure, and so on, but we don't have to think like this – we have the mind of Christ and he never entertained any sinful thoughts. The second part of 2 Corinthians 10:5 says, 'we take captive every thought to make it obedient to Christ'. This is something that's worth practising regularly. Bring* every *thought under the Lord's control. If you do this, you will probably find that you shouldn't be giving thought-time to some of them, so out they go! This will mean less clutter in your mind, leaving more room to think the thoughts which are consistent with a pure heart. In this, as in the other beatitudes, the Lord doesn't pull any punches, does he? He tells it as it is – what you see is what you get. Can the same be said of you? Of me? Or is there just a little too much play-acting in our lives which muddies our purity of heart and blurs our vision of God? I think we both know the answer.*

# 8| The peacemakers

'Blessed are the peacemakers, for they will be called sons of God.'
Matthew 5:9

*The sequence of thought from purity of heart to peacemaking is natural, because one of the most frequent causes of conflict is intrigue, while openness and sincerity are essential to all true reconciliation.*
John Stott [1]

How good are your relationships just now? Perhaps some are moving along quite nicely, whereas others ... well ... you wonder whether 'relationship' is really the right word for what might be going on between you and that other person. Maybe your relationship with him/her has always been rather fragile and you're amazed that, despite all the difficulties, there's still some sort of contact between you; or perhaps you used to get on with each other really well in the past, but more recently you've felt the relationship has started to turn sour and there's often an 'atmosphere' when you're together. Are you prepared to take the risky step of being a peacemaker in this situation? Are you the kind of Christian who builds bridges across rivers of pride, hostility, and misunderstanding, in an attempt to bring about a lasting reconciliation? Jesus Christ was the ultimate reconciler when he became the bridge which spanned the huge chasm between God and sinful people, making it possible for them to turn from their sins and put their trust in him to bring them safely into God's kingdom.

## What does it mean to be peacemakers?

*God custom-designed you with your unique combination of personality, temperament, talents, and background, and He wants to harness and use these in His mission to reach this messed-up world.*
Bill Hybels and Mark Mittelberg [2]

The ultimate peacemaker is God. He went as far as he could to close the gap which existed between him and human beings. God was the One who took the initiative in drawing up the plan of salvation which provides the way for a sinful person to have peace with him.

**Read Romans 5:10; Colossians 1:19–23**

Q Write down, in your own words, what each verse is saying.

One way in which we can help to make peace between God and people is through what 2 Corinthians 5:18 calls 'the ministry of reconciliation'. One example of this is evangelism, which simply means sharing the good news that Jesus came into the world to save sinners. Below are six different evangelistic styles [3] – think about which style you would be most comfortable with. (You might find you fit into more than one of these approaches.)

- Confrontational approach – Peter on the day of Pentecost (Acts 2) – direct, bold and right to the point;
- Intellectual approach – Paul's logical and reasoned presentation of the gospel message eg book of Romans;
- Testimonial approach – blind man (John 9) – your own personal story of becoming a Christian;
- Interpersonal approach – Matthew (Luke 5:29) – investing time in building a relationship;
- Invitational approach – Samaritan woman (John 4) – the kind of person who invites others to a church service or an outreach event;
- Service approach – Dorcas (Acts 9:36) – lending a helping hand.

Ask God to give you at least one person who, as yet, is not a Christian. Using your chosen style(s), pray for the help of his Spirit as you communicate with this person, trusting God for the outcome.

In addition to making peace with God, making peace with others is a responsibility Christians can't ignore. Sometimes this might need to take priority over even our religious practices.

**Read Matthew 5:23,24**

Q Write down what you learn from these verses.

Verse 23 talks about having to *remember* that someone has something against you – this suggests that we're likely to *forget* that there is someone whom we need to make peace with. Give examples of how this forgetfulness might be demonstrated.

What priority does peacemaking have in your life? Are you prepared to drop what you're doing and take the first step in sorting out what's gone wrong in your relationship with another person? Pray about the most effective way of doing this and then *act*!

# What does it mean to be 'sons of God'?

> *So, they who are peacemakers are 'called the children of God.' They demonstrate to the world in such a way that the very blind must see and the very deaf must hear that God is in them. Oh, that we had enough grace to win this blessed commendation! If God has brought you far enough, my reader, to hunger and thirst for righteousness, I pray you never cease your hunger until He has brought you so far as to be a peacemaker, in order that you may be called a child of God.*
> Charles H Spurgeon [4]

In the original Greek, the use of the word 'sons' conveyed something about a person's character eg James and John were called 'sons of thunder' (Mark 3:17), and Barnabas was a nickname which meant 'son of encouragement' (Acts 4:36). In calling peacemakers 'sons of God', no gender distinction is implied, but rather the fact that they mirror the peacemaking character of God.

As a child of God, do you reflect the family likeness as far as peacemaking is concerned? Would people know what 'family' you belonged to just by observing your behaviour as you relate to others? What steps might you need to take to sharpen your likeness to your heavenly Father?

As a child, there were times when I went to speak to my father when he was working in the garden shed. I can't remember him ever telling me to go away because he was too busy – I, along with my sister, had the privilege of being able to interrupt him solely because we were his children. Similarly, we're able to speak to our heavenly Father at any time because we're privileged to be his children.

**Read Matthew 6:9–15**

Q Notice the prayer begins with God being addressed as 'Our Father...' Which of the remaining verses are closely connected to being a peacemaker? What do you think is the relationship between calling God our Father and making peace with others?

**Read Acts 11:26**

Q To be *called* 'sons of God' means that we are known as belonging to him. In Acts we read that 'the disciples were *called* Christians first at Antioch'. Can you give an example, from your own experience or from a book you've read, of a person whose peacemaking behaviour caused him/her to be recognised as one who belonged to God's family?

# Live It Out!

> *The letter [of Paul to Philemon] is personal and focuses on one basic issue: making peace in the Body between two people who have had their relationship broken. It is a beautiful example of the members of the Body of Christ at work to restore broken relationships, and it provides a model for us of keeping peace between ourselves and the people closest to us.*
> Paul Borthwick [5]

We've seen that God is the ultimate peacemaker because he sent Jesus to bridge the gap between the holiness of God and the sinfulness of human beings. By turning from sin to God and trusting that Jesus is sufficient to bring us into a right relationship with him, we will know peace with God. We've also commented on the importance of making peace with other people. In this section, I'd like us to concentrate on the *practical* aspects of being a peacemaker. Are you ready for action?

Making peace where there is none is no easy task – sometimes it might not be possible at all (Romans 12:18); other times it takes a great deal of effort (Romans 14:19). The New Testament book of Philemon is a short, personal letter about the need for peace to be made between two people. The three main characters are Paul (the writer of the letter), Philemon (the slave owner) and Onesimus (the runaway slave). Read the book of Philemon and describe how each of these men brought peace to a troubled relationship.

Their behaviour is an example of Christian fellowship in action. All three men were believers in the Lord (after running away from Philemon, Onesimus responded to the good news of Jesus and became a Christian).

In your relationships with other Christians, what practical steps could you take to act as a peacemaker?

If you're presently at loggerheads with someone, an essential ingredient in learning to be a peacemaker is being prepared to forgive that person. We saw in chapter 6 that merciful people sometimes need to show forgiveness as well as compassion. So, when it comes to being peacemakers, they've already had practice at being forgiving. Ways which indicate true forgiveness might involve looking to how you can help a person who has offended you; or praying that the offending person will become a Christian/will develop a closer relationship with the Lord. Can you think of any other ways of demonstrating forgiveness in action?

Is there someone whom you're not making peace with because you're refusing to forgive that person? Perhaps you've already tried, or the person is continuing in their offence against you and you feel that forgiveness is out of the question. Look at Matthew 18:21,22 – Jesus says there should be no limit to the number of times we forgive someone. Forgiveness will not come naturally – ask the Lord, and keep on asking him, to give you a spirit of forgiveness to the one who is the cause of your pain.

One of the books which I've found very helpful in writing this study is

*Walk This Way – An Interactive Guide To Following Jesus* by Tim Woodroof. 6 The following is taken from his book and shows the significance of the order in which the beatitudes were first taught. Woodroof uses 'relationship language' as he applies the first six beatitudes to a relationship that's gone wrong and needs to be salvaged. This is what he writes:

> *Poverty of spirit makes it possible to confess, 'I was wrong.'*
> *Mourning teaches us to say, 'I'm sorry; please forgive me.'*
> *Meekness causes us to ask, 'What is God's will here?'*
> *A hunger for righteousness leads us to affirm, 'I want to do what's right.'*
> *The quality of mercy drives us to inquire: 'What do you need?'*
> *Purity allows us to promise, 'I'll be honest with you.'*

Bear these comments in mind as you imagine the following scenarios.

- Christine grew up in an abusive home. She is now a Christian. Her mother died several years ago and she hasn't seen her father since then. She is concerned to make contact with him in the hope that there can be peace between them. Beginning with poverty of spirit and ending with purity of heart, how might Christine use the 'relationship language' mentioned above in her attempt to be a peacemaker?
- Mark and Jenny have been Christian believers for many years and had what seemed to be a good marriage relationship. Both are ambitious and have good career opportunities. Pressure of work meant that they were spending more and more time apart and less and less time talking. A rift has developed between them and now, when they do have time in each other's company, they seem to spend most of it arguing and bickering. How might Mark and Jenny use relationship language to make peace in their situation?
- John works for Mr Green who is a difficult boss. Mr Green loves to make fun of people whose views are different from his own. Soon after he employed John, he discovered that John was a Christian, and this seems to have fuelled his liking for ridicule – in fact, Mr Green is often openly hostile in his remarks to John about his beliefs. This has led to a strained atmosphere between the two men. How might John use relationship language in an attempt to make peace with Mr Green?

Can you identify a situation in your own life where you could apply the relationship language we've just been considering? Ask the Lord to give you the wisdom and guidance which you need as you do your part in making peace in a troubled relationship.

> *If you have a broken relationship, make certain that you have done and are doing everything you can to mend it. Don't let yourself off the hook easily. Go the extra mile, humble yourself, initiate the reconciliation, be willing to swallow your pride… whatever it takes for true reconciliation … For those who've done all you can to be reconciled and the other person refuses, don't live in false guilt about that relationship. Remember, the principle is, as much as it depends on you, live at peace with all people (Romans 12:18). Many things are out of your control, and that is what you have to accept and trust to God's care.*
> Mary Whelchel [7]

## Personal comment

*Peacemakers – those who are called 'sons of God' – know what it is to be at peace with God. By turning from their sins and trusting in Christ for salvation, such people are the recipients of God's forgiveness and blessing. It doesn't stop there though, does it? If we're at peace with God ourselves, this should make us want to bring others into a relationship of peace with him. There are many different ways we can do this – see the list of evangelistic styles in the first section of this chapter. Are you exercising the style that suits your personality and abilities? By doing so, you could become a peacemaker. You could be the one whom God uses to bring another person into a right relationship with him so that there is peace between them. Or maybe you're like the apostle Paul whose desire was to reconcile Christians who weren't at peace with each other (compare Philippians 4:2,3; Philemon vs 8–11). Do you act as a peacemaker when two or more Christians known to you just aren't getting on together, or do you unwittingly act as a troublemaker by gossiping, taking sides, or critically condemning one or the other? Or what about when you're the one who's not at peace with someone? Whether you're the offender (Matthew 5:23,24) or the offended (Matthew 18:15), the Bible teaches it's up to you to make the first move. Scary stuff! Two important elements in making peace with another are confession and forgiveness. But surely if it's the other person's fault, I don't need to confess anything? Maybe it* is *their fault, but perhaps you contributed to the rift by taking offence at what they did. It could be that you need to confess this to God and to the one you're not at peace with. If you need to forgive this person, be sure that your attitude is right. Luke 17:3 begins with 'So watch yourselves ...' and then goes on to talk about forgiving the repentant person. Matthew 7:3–5 warns against focusing on another's faults before we're prepared to deal ruthlessly with our own. But, someone might say, how can I forgive and forget when I've been so badly hurt? Nowhere in the Bible are we ever commanded to 'forgive and forget' – only God does that (see Hebrews 8:12). Although we might never forget what someone has done against us, part of forgiving them means that we don't raise the issue with them again. Neither do we continue talking about it to a third party or go on brooding over the offence. How ready are you to be a peacemaker by forgiving a person who has hurt you? If you're not yet willing to forgive him/her, are you willing to be made willing? Perhaps this is the point at which you have to start – ask the Lord to give you the desire to be willing to forgive. These words don't make comfortable reading – it's so much easier to politely avoid the person or to pretend that there isn't really a problem at all, isn't it? Is your Christian life and mine so real and authentic that peacemaking isn't an option, but an unavoidable necessity?*

# 9| Those who are persecuted

'Blessed are those who are persecuted because of righteousness, for theirs is the kingdom of heaven. Blessed are you when people insult you, persecute you and falsely say all kinds of evil against you because of me. Rejoice and be glad, because great is your reward in heaven, for in the same way they persecuted the prophets who were before you.'
Matthew 5:10–12

*Let there be no mistake about this, the righteous will be persecuted – inevitably so. Once we adopt the attitudes and principles which Christ presents so clearly for us in His Sermon on the Mount, the men and women of the world are going to react with hostility and indignation.*
**Selwyn Hughes** [1]

'You're blessed when your commitment to God provokes persecution. The persecution drives you even deeper into God's kingdom.' This is how Eugene Peterson translates Matthew 5:10 in *The Message*. [2] This beatitude is longer than the rest – three verses (10–12) compared to just one for each of the other seven. It's also different from the rest because it doesn't describe what Christian disciples should be like, but rather how they are treated by others as a result of living out the principles of all the other beatitudes put together. The climax of beatitude living is ... persecution. But why are they persecuted? Verses 10 and 11 tell us it's because of righteousness and because of Jesus, the One whom they follow. Persecution for any other reason eg self-righteousness or wrongdoing, doesn't lead to the promise of a heavenly kingdom and heavenly rewards. The Christian's response to all this? Verse 12 says it is to 'rejoice and be glad'. If we were to ask the general public how people should respond to unjust persecution, do you think the answer would be to leap for joy? I doubt it. Once again, Jesus' teaching goes against the grain of our natural way of thinking.

# What does it mean to be persecuted because of righteousness?

> *The words 'persecuted for righteousness' sake' and 'for My sake' (King James Version) caution us to see to it that we are opposed and hated* **solely** *because we are the followers of the Lord Jesus, and not on account of our own misconduct or injudicious behaviour (see 1 Peter 2:19–24).*
> Arthur W Pink [3]

Several verses in the Bible warn us about the reality of persecution for Christian believers. Three of these verses are given below. What do you learn from them?

**Read John 15:20; Philippians 1:29; 2 Timothy 3:12**

Matthew 5:11 describes persecution or harassment in three ways:

- Insults – verbal abuse, characterised by unkind, taunting, mocking words
- Persecution – from a Greek word meaning to pursue, harass, trouble, or molest
- False accusations – lies, slander, damaging a person's reputation.

Give practical examples of each type of harassment.

**Read 1 Corinthians 4:12,13**

Q What are the similarities between these verses and Matthew 5:11?

This beatitude doesn't just say, 'Blessed are those who are persecuted, for theirs is the kingdom of heaven.' It gives the reason for the persecution – 'because of righteousness'. In other words, the persecuted ones who are blessed or favoured by God are those, *and only those,* who are living for

God and following the Lord Jesus. Make a list of attitudes and/or behaviours displayed by some Christians which might lead to persecution which has nothing to do with genuinely living for God.

Matthew 5:12 refers to 'the prophets' who suffered persecution. There are many prophets mentioned in the Bible who suffered at the hands of those who were opposed to them and their message. Daniel, for example, was persecuted by foreign powers and authorities whereas Jeremiah suffered as a direct result of vindictive treatment meted out by his own people. The apostle Paul was insulted by people in the church (2 Corinthians 10 and 11) and the Lord Jesus was betrayed by one of his own disciples. Do you think that experiencing persecution from those who claim to be Christian believers is more difficult to bear than persecution from any other source? Give an explanation for your answer.

Are you going through a time of persecution right now? Does it involve a group of people or an individual whom you thought you could trust? Sometimes even those who say they are Christians respond negatively when brought face to face with the life of someone who takes Jesus' teaching seriously. If you're on the receiving end of abusive treatment because you're living for God, give thanks to him that this confirms you're living as you should be and use this as an opportunity to shine for the Lord all the more brightly.

> *Suffering, then, is the badge of true discipleship. The disciple is not above his master... Discipleship means allegiance to the suffering Christ, and it is not at all surprising that Christians should be called upon to suffer. In fact, it is a joy and a token of His grace.*
> Dietrich Bonhoeffer [4]

## What is your reward in heaven?

> *Those who trust in Jesus have what the Bible calls an inheritance. They're written into God's will, and one day when that will is settled, they will all share in His wonderful estate. According to Jesus, all this has been 'prepared for you since the creation of the world' (Matthew 25:34). Paul encourages us that 'our present sufferings are not worth comparing with the glory that will be revealed in us'*

*(Romans 8:18). When times are hard, that's comforting to know. While your feet are planted firmly in this world, stop and think about the next one. It's there; it's going to be wonderful; and it can make a difference in your life today.*
Kevin Miller [5]

You'll notice that Matthew 5:10 promises the kingdom of heaven as the blessing to those who are persecuted because of righteousness. This is the same promise made at the beginning to those who are poor in spirit. People just starting out in the Christian life are as much citizens of the kingdom of heaven as seasoned believers whose close walk with the Lord has led to a beatitude lifestyle. In verse 12, though, Jesus adds another promise for those who suffer because of their relationship to him – 'Great is your reward in heaven ...' Several verses in the Bible talk about heavenly rewards.

**Read Matthew 16:27; Revelation 22:12; James 1:12; Hebrews 11:26**

Q Paraphrase each verse

Q How might the knowledge that 'great is your reward in heaven' help you to cope with being harassed for your faithfulness to the Lord's teachings here and now?

Q Try to imagine what your great reward in heaven might be and then read 1 Corinthians 2:9. How does this verse encourage you as you look forward to your heavenly reward?

As you think about the Lord's promise of a reward for you in heaven, thank him that he knows what you're presently going through as you live for him here and now. Remind yourself that Jesus was no stranger to persecution, and take comfort and encouragement from 1 Peter 4:12–19.

# Live It Out!

*We are blessed when we are persecuted, because persecution means that we have been seen. That we have been heard. That our actions have been taken note of by the powers that be and have made their mark. That we have done something right enough, for a change, to deserve persecution. Something that puts us in the same class as the prophets whom Jesus so honoured for their faith and courage. Something that puts us in the same class as Jesus himself, who suffered persecution.*
Ralph F Wilson 6

So, the peacemaker becomes the persecuted. Are you surprised? The question we need to tackle now is 'How should I respond when I'm on the receiving end of taunts, harassment and lies which come as a direct result of living for God?'

Matthew gives an astounding answer – 'rejoice and be glad'. Luke says '... leap for joy ...' What is your initial reaction when you read these words?

**Read Matthew 5:12; Luke 6:23**

Q Why should we rejoice and be glad in the face of persecution? Try to give at least two reasons.

Read the verses in the following table and write down their recommendations for responding to persecution.

| Verses | Suggested responses |
|---|---|
| Romans 12:14 | |
| 1 Corinthians 4:12,13 | |
| 2 Timothy 2:3 | |
| Hebrews 12:2,3 | |
| James 1:2–4 | |
| 1 Peter 3:9 | |
| 1 Peter 4:12–16 | |

Take at least one of these verses or passages and share with your group *practical* ways in which they could be applied.

Take your chosen verse(s) and make a decision to live out these recommendations in your own particular circumstances. Ask for the Lord's help in this and trust him to give you all the obedience, strength and self-control which you need to put his Word into practice.

In our country at the present time, we know nothing of being imprisoned and tortured for our faithfulness to the Lord. This isn't the case in some other countries, however. In various parts of the world, Christians are being physically persecuted *today* because they choose to stay true to the name of Christ. Ways in which we can help these people might involve the following:

- Writing letters to Christians imprisoned for their faith
- Regularly praying for named individuals and their families who are suffering persecution
- Subscribing to a free newsletter or magazine of a relief agency
- Helping to supply Bibles to Christians who don't have any
- Organising an event to raise funds for the persecuted church

Further details of how people in this situation can be supported are available from various agencies, eg Open Doors International (www.od.org) or The Voice of the Martyrs (www.persecution.com). As a group, choose at least one of these items and make a firm commitment to act on this without delay. If necessary, appoint someone from your group who will action your decision. Don't be satisfied with a 'one-off' response – the needs of persecuted Christians are ongoing. Be prepared to address this issue again and again as a group.

What is your personal response to the needs of Christians in other countries suffering appalling abuse and ill-treatment? Ask the Lord how he wants you to respond and look for ways in which you could really make a difference in the life of a persecuted Christian.

## Personal comment

*She came out of the Christian book shop wearing her new bracelet with the initials 'WWJD' embroidered on it. This was to remind her to stop and ask the question 'What Would Jesus Do?' whenever she was faced with a tricky situation. Jesus, of course, would always do the right thing, but there's a sense in which we can't be absolutely sure how exactly he would do the right thing. Similarly, can we know with certainty precisely what he would say in response to a particular question? When he talked face to face with people during his life on earth, he often astounded them by what he said. His recommendations in Matthew 5:12 and in Luke 6:23 were no exception. It must have been quite mind-boggling to be told to 'rejoice and be glad' or 'leap for joy' when you're faced with different varieties of persecution solely because you're living in the way he told you to!*

*Why did Jesus tell his harassed people to respond in this way? I think there are several reasons. Firstly, it's a response that's unnatural. When Christians are joyful in the face of opposition, it speaks volumes about the reality of their relationship with the Lord. No one is naturally full of joy when hard times come. The strength to be joyful in such circumstances has to come from a source outside themselves. Secondly, Christians can be joyful when persecuted for right living because this means that God considers them worthy to suffer for him (see Acts 5:41). Thirdly, suffering can have a positive effect on Christian development (see Romans 5:3,4) and, fourthly, it can give opportunities for the good news of Jesus Christ to be communicated in situations that would otherwise be impossible as when Christians are imprisoned for their faithfulness to the Lord. The apostle Paul used his prison experiences to write letters which are now part of the Bible, and his joyful response to hardship in prison led to the conversion of the jailer in Philippi. The Romanian pastor, Richard Wurmbrand, spent fourteen years in a communist prison because of his faith, yet he led many of his fellow-prisoners to salvation in Christ. 'Rejoice and be glad' and 'leap for joy' in the face of persecution – how well do we measure up?*

# 10| Finishing touches

'And we... are being transformed into his likeness
with ever-increasing glory.'

2 Corinthians 3:18

*The Beatitudes are from start to finish a riddle, a paradox, a series of riddles. The world admires them as great literature and as a statement of ideals held in honour, but denies the possibility of their actual fulfillment... But with the Spirit of Jesus within us, literally, we can and must live out these Beatitudes as a testimony to our world of the Living Christ.*

**Ralph F Wilson** 1

I think it's good to read a familiar bible passage in different versions as this can often make it seem fresher and more alive. One translation which fits into this category is *The Message* by Eugene Peterson. Below is Matthew 5:1-12 taken from this source.

*When Jesus saw his ministry drawing huge crowds, he climbed a hillside. Those who were apprenticed to him, the committed, climbed with him. Arriving at a quiet place, he sat down and taught his climbing companions. This is what he said:*

*"You're blessed when you're at the end of your rope. With less of you there is more of God and his rule.*

*"You're blessed when you feel you've lost what is most dear to you. Only then can you be embraced by the One most dear to you.*

*"You're blessed when you're content with just who you are – no more, no less. That's the moment you find yourselves proud owners of everything that can't be bought.*

*"You're blessed when you've worked up a good appetite for God. He's food and drink in the best meal you'll ever eat.*

> *"You're blessed when you care. At the moment of being 'care-full', you find yourselves cared for.*
>
> *"You're blessed when you get your inside world – your mind and heart – put right. Then you can see God in the outside world.*
>
> *"You're blessed when you can show people how to cooperate instead of compete or fight. That's when you discover who you really are, and your place in God's family.*
>
> *"You're blessed when your commitment to God provokes persecution. The persecution drives you deeper into God's kingdom.*
>
> *"Not only that – count yourselves blessed every time people put you down or throw you out or speak lies about you to discredit me. What it means is that the truth is too close for comfort and they are uncomfortable. You can be glad when that happens – give a cheer even! – for though they don't like it, I do! And all heaven applauds. And know that you are in good company. My prophets and witnesses have always gotten into this kind of trouble."* [2]

Has this study made any practical difference to the way you live? Have you progressed at all in your spiritual journey? One of the main purposes of Bible studies is to help bring about a lasting change for the better in the people who've done the studies. How true is this of you? Let's use the first part of this chapter to review what's been learned from earlier chapters.

## Let's review!

Look back over all the previous chapters of this study and, in the following table, write down the main principles learned and how you've been able to apply them to your life in a practical way.

| Chapter | Principles learned | How applied |
|---|---|---|
| *1* | | |
| *2* | | |
| *3* | | |
| *4* | | |
| *5* | | |
| *6* | | |
| *7* | | |
| *8* | | |
| *9* | | |

Which of these chapters did you find particularly difficult? Share with your group the reasons for your answer.

Which chapters did you find particularly helpful? Share your answer with the rest of your group.

> *A deep happiness can be ours in the midst of poverty, in the face of sorrow, in the position of weakness. We value righteousness and are rewarded. We show mercy and receive it in return. We live in purity and meet the Purifier. We spread peace and are known by God's name. And if life's worst befalls us, even then the King himself is with us; his Kingdom belongs to us.*
> James Patrick Long [3]

# Who is the model for this portrait?

> *Each of the promises of the beatitudes finds its accomplishment in Christ. Poor in spirit He was, and His supremely is the Kingdom. Mourn He did, yet He will be comforted as He sees of the travail of His soul (Isaiah 53:11). He was meekness personified, yet He is now seated upon a throne of glory. He hungered and thirsted after righteousness, yet now He is filled with satisfaction as He beholds that the righteousness which He worked out has been imputed to His people. Pure in heart, He sees God as none other sees Him (Matthew 11:27). As the Peacemaker, He is acknowledged as the unique Son of God by all the blood-bought children. As the persecuted One, great is His reward, for He has been given the name above all others (Philippians 2:9-11).*
> **A W Pink** 4

One of the greatest purposes which God has for Christian believers is for them 'to be conformed to the likeness of his Son' (Romans 8:29) and in 2 Corinthians 3:18 we read that we 'are being transformed into his likeness...'. God wants you and me to be like Jesus! In Matthew 5:1–12 we have a portrait of a Christian disciple, and the model for this is the Lord Jesus Christ. Each characteristic of the beatitudes is a reflection of some aspect of the personality of Jesus.

**Read Matthew 26:67; Mark 14:36; John 4:34; 2 Corinthians 8:9; Colossians 1:20; Hebrews 2:17; 5:7; 7:26**

Q Write down what each verse says and the beatitude to which it is linked.

Has this study encouraged you to want to be more like Jesus? None of us can be completely like him in this life, but remind yourself of Romans 8:29 and 2 Corinthians 3:18. Take time now to thank the Lord that he wants to make something out of your life – are you prepared to reflect his characteristics as you go about your daily routine? Allow the Lord to paint your portrait in his colours and the finished result will be a true likeness to Jesus.

# Do you have a cross-shaped lifestyle?

> *The possibility of losing their lives was very real for the disciples as well as for Jesus. Real discipleship implies real commitment – pledging our whole existence to his service... If we protect ourselves from the pain God calls us to suffer, we begin to die spiritually and emotionally. Our lives turn inward, and we lose our intended purpose. When we give our life in service to Christ, however, we discover the real purpose of living.*
> **Life Application Study Bible** [5]

In Matthew 16:24 Jesus says, 'If any of you wants to be my follower, you must put aside your selfish ambition, shoulder your cross, and follow me'. (New Living Translation). Have you ever wondered what's meant by shouldering your cross? In Roman times, criminals who were condemned to death by crucifixion had to carry their own cross to the place of execution. It was heavy, often difficult, and was carried in the full glare of any onlookers. Beatitude living can be like this too – some of its demands can be heavy eg mourning over our sins; it is often difficult eg showing mercy when you'd rather strike out; and it's played out in the glare of public scrutiny – we live as disciples in the real world, where our thoughts and motives are translated into behaviour which can be seen by everyone we meet. Perhaps it's no coincidence, then, that beatitude living is cross-shaped, with the first four beatitudes forming the vertical bar and the remaining four forming the horizontal bar. From your own experience, how has living a beatitude lifestyle sometimes involved you having to 'shoulder your cross'?

The following verse, Matthew 16:25, says: 'If you try to keep your life for yourself, you will lose it'. In what specific ways is it possible to 'keep your life for yourself'?

Jesus goes on in the rest of the verse to say: 'But if you give up your life for me, you will find true life'. In what specific ways might living a beatitude lifestyle involve giving up your life for the Lord?

In this context, what do you understand by the phrase 'you will find true life'?

Have your answers to any of these questions helped you to view 'shouldering your cross' in a more positive light? Remember that God's purpose is to make you like Jesus, and the cross was central to his life. Give thanks to the Lord that he didn't resist dying on the cross for your sins. Perhaps you've completed this Bible study and have never made a personal response to Jesus' life, death and resurrection. Maybe you've thought that living to the best of your ability was all that could be expected of you. Possibly you still haven't appreciated that the blessings promised in the beatitudes are only for those who've confessed their sins to the Lord and turned from them. If so, will you take time now to hand your life over to him so that he can forgive you and make you clean? You might find it helpful to pray in the following way. Carefully consider what you're saying as you pray.

> 'Heavenly Father, thank you that your Son, Jesus, came to this world to die for sinners. I confess that I'm a sinner – I've turned my back on you and gone my own way. I realise now that I can't make it on my own. I realise that I need to be made clean from all my sins and that you are the only one who can do this for me. I believe that Jesus had to die on the cross at Calvary so that his blood which poured out could make me clean. I come to you with all the sin, shame and guilt which has built up in my life and I ask you to completely forgive me and make me

new. Help me to depend on you to do this and give me the desire to turn my back on everything which isn't pleasing to you. I need your help to live as one of your followers – a disciple – by regularly reading your word, the Bible, and allowing you to change me more and more into the person you want me to be. Make me enthusiastic about talking often to you in prayer – praising you for who you are; confessing my daily sins; thanking you for all you've done and are doing; and praying on behalf of others. Help me to meet regularly with other Christians for worship and Bible study so that I'll learn more about you and how I can best live for you from day to day. In Jesus' name, amen.'

If you've prayed this prayer with all sincerity and honesty, it's important that you tell another Christian that you've done this as soon as possible. This is often the simplest way of telling someone that you're now a Christian believer. Don't leave it there, though. If you haven't already done so, find a church where God's word is faithfully taught week by week. Make yourself known to the Christians there. Speak to the leadership about your baptism – the church's public identification, recognition and affirmation of the Christian believer. Look for opportunities where you can make a useful contribution to the life of that church. Begin the excellent habit of reading the Bible every day – the gospel of John is a good place to start. You might then want to follow a Bible reading plan – many of them can be adapted to suit your own individual needs. Ask at your local Christian bookshop for details. Get into the practice of praying on a daily basis too – find a place where you're unlikely to be disturbed and talk to God. To get you started, you might want to use what's called 'the Lord's prayer' as a model on which to build your own prayers – see Matthew 6:9–13. Incidentally, this is more properly 'the disciples' prayer' as they were the ones whom the Lord was teaching to pray. Don't be afraid to let people know that you're a Christian and don't worry that you don't have all the answers – none of us do! Don't get discouraged when you find that you're not perfect – as soon as you realise you've sinned, confess it to the Lord who has promised that he will go on making you clean (1 John 1:9). As you release more and more of your life to him by obeying what he says in the Bible and submitting to his control, you'll find that the Holy Spirit (who lives in every Christian believer) will guide and empower you in the various situations you face. Welcome to the world of the 'blessed' people!

> *We enter the kingdom through the new birth (John 3:1–16), but we enjoy the kingdom by living for those things that please God the most (Matthew 6:33). The world (and worldly believers) would disagree with Christ's description of a blessed person, but the description is true just the same. God majors on character, and so should we.*
> **Warren W Wiersbe** [6]

# Personal Comment

*Have you ever had your portrait painted? My mother did a fair bit of oil painting as a hobby and she decided that she wanted to produce a painting of me. The sittings involved were often tedious and because I wasn't supposed to move, I wanted to move all the more! And the more I protested about having to keep still, the longer I had to sit! In this study, we've looked at God's portrait of what he wants his disciples to look like. How do you and I measure up? Are there times when you don't want to sit still before Him but would rather be busy doing your own thing? In order for him to produce a good likeness to Jesus, there will be times when you'll need to sit quietly in his presence and tune in to how he wants you to live. Rushing about frantically here and there, being ever so busy, doesn't make you like Jesus. Do you remember the story of Martha and Mary in Luke 10:38-42? Read this passage again and take note of what each of the sisters was doing – which woman did Jesus commend?*

*There were times when I didn't like the look of my painting in its unfinished state and I would have loved to have taken the brush from my mother and substituted my own choice of colours for the ones she had used. However, my mother was the expert and she knew what she was doing. Do you sometimes protest about the colours the Lord is using in his portrait of a disciple? Do they seem too harsh to you? Would you rather that he didn't use so many dark shades? Are you longing for lighter and brighter colours in your life? Remember that the dark shades are just as necessary in your portrait as the bright colours. A painting which was all bright would lack depth and variety.*

*Anytime I complained that the painting didn't look like me at all, my mother would say, 'But it's not finished yet!' When the painting was finally completed, it was a very good likeness and the colours she'd used seemed just right. We often don't like what the Lord is doing with us, do we? We forget that he's 'not finished yet' and that we 'are* being *transformed into his likeness' (2*

*Corinthians 3:18). The portrait of a disciple isn't painted overnight – it's a slow process for us to become like Jesus, and the Artist doesn't rush because he wants to make something beautiful out of our imperfect lives. Will you allow him to make you like Jesus? If so, then why not commit yourself to the cross-shaped beatitude lifestyle?*

# Endnotes

## Chapter 1

1 Tim Woodroof, *Walk This Way – An Interactive Guide To Following Jesus*, NavPress, 1999, p25.

2 John Blanchard, *The Beatitudes for Today*, Day One Publications, 1999, p27.

3 John Stott, *The Message of The Sermon on the Mount*, IVP, 1978, p31.

4 Ralph F Wilson, *Lesson 1, The Beatitudes, Matthew 5:1–12*, Joyful Heart Ministries (www.joyfulheart.com/manifesto/lesson1-e.htm).

5 A W Pink, *The Beatitudes – Introduction* (www.pbtseminary.com/books/pink/Beatitudes/bea_intro.htm)

## Chapter 2

1 J David Hoke, *The Poor In Spirit – Matthew 5:3*. See www.horizonsnet.org

2 Mary Whelchel, 'Christmas in the Marketplace', *The Christian Working Woman*, Monday 18 December 2000. (This organisation broadcasts in the USA and elsewhere. See www.christianworkingwoman.org for transcripts.)

3 Harold Camping, Transcript 130C – *Blessed are the Poor in Spirit* from The Open Forum with Harold Camping. www.ozemail.com.au/~lkolberg/transcripts/C130C.html

4 Bill Dodds and Michael J Dodds, *Living The Beatitudes Today*, Loyola Press, 1997, p27.

## Chapter 3

1 Tim Woodroof, *Walk This Way – An Interactive Guide To Following Jesus*, NavPress, 1999, p57.

2 John Blanchard, *The Beatitudes for Today*, Day One Publications, 1999, pp96,99.

3 John Blanchard, *The Beatitudes for Today*, Day One Publications, 1999.

4 *Life Application Study Bible: New Living Translation*, Tyndale House, 1996, p904.
5 A W Pink, *The Beatitudes – The Second Beatitude.* (www.pbtseminary.com/books/pink/Beatitudes/bea_02.htm)
6 Warren and Ruth Myers, *Praise – A Door to God's Presence*, NavPress, 1987, p153.

## Chapter 4

1 Bill Dodds and Michael J Dodds, *Living the Beatitudes Today*, Loyola Press, 1997, p60.
2 Tim Woodroof, *Walk This Way – An Interactive Guide To Following Jesus*, NavPress, 1999, p76.
3 Tim Woodroof, *Walk This Way – An Interactive Guide To Following Jesus*, NavPress, 1999, p77.
4 Charles Spurgeon, *God Will Bless You*, Whitaker House, 1997, p52.
5 Charles Spurgeon, *God Will Bless You*, Whitaker House, 1997, p60.
6 Elisabeth Elliot, *A Heart for God* (Perpetual Calendar), July 19, from *Fitting Into My Sphere* (audio cassette).
7 John Blanchard, *The Beatitudes for Today*, Day One Publications, 1999, p135.

## Chapter 5

1 Charles Spurgeon, *God Will Bless You*, Whitaker House, 1997, p63.
2 Spiros Zodhiates, *The Beatitudes: The Pursuit of Happiness*, AMG International, 1998, p346.
3 Mary Whelchel, *What Is Spoiling Your Appetite?* The Christian Working Woman – a nationwide radio ministry, Thursday 17 August 2000. (This organisation broadcasts in the USA and elsewhere. See www.christianworkingwoman.org for transcripts.)
4 Spiros Zodhiates, *The Beatitudes: The Pursuit of Happiness*, AMG International, 1998, p347.
5 *Life Application Study Bible: New Living Translation*, Tyndale House, 1996, p2051.
6 A W Tozer, *The Pursuit of God*, Christian Publications, 1982, p23.

## Chapter 6

1 Tim Woodroof, *Walk This Way – an Interactive Guide to Following Jesus*, NavPress, 1999, p131.

2 John Blanchard, *The Beatitudes for Today*, Day One Publications, 1999, p170.

3 *Life Application Study Bible: New Living Translation*, Tyndale House, 1996, p1462.

4 Kathy Johnston, 'Ministers of Mercy', *Discipleship Journal*, no. 36 (Nov/Dec 1986). (Text taken from CD Rom, published by NavPress. Visit www.discipleshipjournal.org for details.)

5 Warren Wiersbe, *Live Like a King: Developing a Royal Lifestyle from the Beatitudes*, Kregel Publications, 1995, pp105,106. Used with permission.

6 Mary Whelchel, *If You Only Knew*, Cook Communications Ministries, 1996. Used with permission. All rights reserved.

## Chapter 7

1 Gary L Thomas, 'Pure Refreshment', *Discipleship Journal*, no.116 (Mar/Apr 2000), p44.

2 John Stott, *The Message of the Sermon on the Mount*, IVP, 1978, p49.

3 Mary Whelchel, *What Would Jesus Think?* Cook Communications Ministries, 1998. P110. Used with permission. All rights reserved.

4 Tim Woodroof, *Walk This Way – an Interactive Guide to Following Jesus*, NavPress, 1999, p200.

5 Adam R Holz, 'Letting Go Of Lust', *Discipleship Journal*, no.116 (Mar/Apr 2000), p68.

## Chapter 8

1 John Stott, *The Message of the Sermon on the Mount*, IVP, 1978, p50.

2 Bill Hybels and Mark Mittelberg, *Becoming a Contagious Christian*, Zondervan, 1994, chapter 9, 'Finding the Approach that fits you'.

3 Bill Hybels and Mark Mittelberg, *Becoming a Contagious Christian*, Zondervan, 1994, p122.

4 Charles H Spurgeon, *God Will Bless You*, Whitaker House, 1997, p169.

5 Paul Borthwick, 'Conflict in the Body,' *Discipleship Journal*, no. 31 (Jan/Feb 1986). (Text taken from CD Rom, published by NavPress. Visit www.discipleshipjournal.org for details.)

6 Tim Woodroof, *Walk This Way – An Interactive Guide to Following Jesus,* NavPress, 1999.

7 Mary Whelchel, 'Dealing With Broken Relationships' – a radio broadcast of *The Christian Working Woman,* 11 February 1999. (This organisation broadcasts in the USA and elsewhere.
See www.christianworkingwoman.org for transcripts.)

## Chapter 9

1 Selwyn Hughes, *The Divine Attitudes,* CWR, 1989.

2 Eugene Peterson, *The Message – The New Testament in Contemporary Language,* NavPress, 1993, p16.

3 A W Pink, *The Beatitudes – The Eighth Beatitude*
(www.pbtseminary.com/books/pink/Beatitudes/bea_08.htm)

4 Dietrich Bonhoeffer, *The Cost of Discipleship,* SCM, 1959, p81.

5 Kevin A Miller, 'Heaven Can't Wait' *Discipleship Journal* no. 57 (May/June 1990). (Text taken from CD Rom, published by NavPress.
Visit www.discipleshipjournal.org for details.)

6 Ralph F Wilson, *Lesson 1 – The Beatitudes.*
See www.joyfulheart.com/manifesto/lesson1–e.htm

## Chapter 10

1 Ralph F Wilson *Lesson 1 – The Beatitudes.*
See www.joyfulheart.com/manifesto/lesson1–e.htm

2 Eugene Peterson *The Message – The New Testament in Contemporary Language,* NavPress, 1993, pp15,16.

3 James Patrick Long 'The Incongruous Kingdom', *Discipleship Journal,* no 68 (March/April 1992). (Text taken from CD Rom, published by NavPress.
Visit www.discipleshipjournal.org for details.)

4 A W Pink *The Beatitudes – Conclusion*
www.pbtseminary.com/books/pink/Beatitudes/bea_conclusion.htm

5 *Life Application Study Bible: New Living Translation,* Tyndale House Publishers Inc, 1996, p1442.

6 Warren W Wiersbe *With The Word – The Chapter-by-Chapter Bible Handbook,* Thomas Nelson Publishers, p634.

# Other Resources from Scripture Union

## Bodybuilders

Small group resource

A highly relational small group resource that's flexible and fun to use. Six outlines in each book contain notes for leaders, prayer and worship ideas, photocopiable sheets of interactive and in-depth Bible study material and ideas for personal study during the week.

***A Fresh Encounter*** (David Bolster) 1 85999 586 1

***Designed for Great Things*** (Anton Bauhmohl) 1 85999 585 3

***Living for the King*** ('Tricia Williams) 1 85999 584 5

***Relationship Building*** (Lance Pierson) 1 85999 582 9

***Surviving Under Pressure*** (Christopher Griffiths & Stephen Hathway) 1 85999 587 X

***Growing Through Change*** (Lance Pierson) 1 85999 583 7

210x140mm pb 32pp £3.50

## Journey into the Bible

John Drane

ISBN: 1 85999 409 1, £4.99

In his usual thought-provoking and accessible style John Drane gives a stimulating introduction to many of the issues raised by reading the Bible today. Designed especially for those who are struggling to come to terms with the Bible.

## Understanding the Bible

John Stott

A format pb 192pp £2.99

ISBN 1 85999 225 0

A special budget edition of a widely-acclaimed classic bestseller. Outstanding Christian teacher and author John Stott examines the cultural, social, geographical and historical background of the Bible, outlining the story and explaining the message.

## Understanding the Bible

John Stott

245x160mm hb 170pp £9.99

1 85999 569 1

A brand new edition in full colour. Revised and updated text is illustrated with charts, diagrams and wonderful colour photos. An ideal gift!

## Knowing God's Ways

***A user's guide to the Old Testament***

Patton Taylor

ISBN: 1 85999 349 4, £6.99

Do you find the Old Testament difficult to get into? If you've been looking for some help in making sense of it all, then this book by a professor at Union Theological College in Belfast is what you've been looking for! His accessible. user-friendly approach will help you gain a clear overview of the Old Testament, understand different genres, and apply biblical teaching to today's world.